MW00415709

THE OUTHOUSE AT THE END OF THE EARTH

Sherry Day's Story
of Her Challenging Experiences
in a
Remote Papua New Guinean Village

To Hal & Lin - How special it was
to meet you. I hope you enjoy reading
God's story of my life.

By

Sherry Day

Sherry D

© Sherry Day 2012

"It is thou, O king, that art grown and become strong: for thy greatness is grown, and reacheth unto heaven, and thy dominion to the end of the earth."
Daniel 4:22 (KJV)

Biography

Sherry Day has been a missionary since 1987, serving alongside her husband Bill in Papua New Guinea for three-and-a-half years, Belize for nine years, and now in the United States where they work with foreign nationals using ESL (English as a Second Language) as their primary evangelistic tool – continuing their ministry under Mission to the World.

She is a charter member of her sending church, Surfside Presbyterian (PCA), in Surfside Beach, South Carolina. She loves to disciple and equip younger women, staying involved in several ministries that allow her to do so.

Sherry has two biological sons, four step-sons, four adopted Belizean children, several grandchildren, and one great grandchild.

Sherry, her husband and family currently live in Surfside Beach, SC.

Remarks from the Editor

One decade before television launched its first Survivor reality show, Sherry Day, her husband, and two sons were set down in one of the most remote places on earth and told to survive. Their long-term goal was to learn enough about the Faiwol people of Papua New Guinea to launch a literacy support project aimed at teaching the tribe to read their own spoken language. Meanwhile, two fellow missionaries were continuing a painstaking translation of the Bible into Faiwol to eventually allow the people to read the very thoughts of God.

It sounds like an assignment for seasoned veterans, but in fact, Sherry Day was – by her own description – a complete novice and the least likely of candidates. A city girl with a troubled past but a wonderful conversion to Jesus Christ, Sherry had no intention of leaving the United States to work with a tribe whose grandparents were cannibals.

In a wonderful, transparent, laugh-aloud book, Sherry relates her resistance to her husband's escalating sense of being called to be a missionary. There is no sense of self-importance in this story – only a desperate casting of herself on the mercy of God. At the same time, Sherry, Bill, Wade and Chris are clearly people who live large once their die is cast – opening themselves up to new risks and experiences, and growing constantly. This leads to an exciting look at a lifestyle driven by relationship-building instead of clocks, calendars, and salaries.

Sherry's book is personal without being self conscious. She realistically describes her slow acclimatization, and by the end, it is obvious that she has fallen in love with a tribe who – though they may wear nose-bones and modesty gourds – have the same strengths and failings as the members of the "civilized" world, and indeed, more civilized attitudes than many of us.

Even as her editor, I found myself wanting to read the book over and over. I resisted the impulse to make it sound more "literary," because to do so would destroy a clear and innocent voice that subtly calls us to drop our masks and be truthful about our fears – and joyful about the love that God plants in resistant hearts. *The Outhouse at the End of the Earth* is a quietly moving book that strengthened my own faith in the God who calls us to hard things.

Margaret G. Locklair - Conway, SC - July 17, 2009

Acknowledgments

I'm most grateful to the Lord for His patience with me – especially during my first year in Papua New Guinea. His presence in my life changed me dramatically. Where once I had no hope, now I have the hope of eternal life with Him. Where once I felt I would never amount to anything, I know that I can do all things through His Son, Jesus Christ. Where once I felt that I had no worth, I realize that I have great worth because Christ lives in me, and I was planned and created with God's glory and will in mind. In our years in Papua New Guinea, every one of these truths would become vastly richer, indescribably deeper to me.

I dedicate this book first to Bill – my husband, best friend and great love. He, too, had to be patient with me through my whining and growing up. Thank you, Bill, for your love and support.

I also dedicate this book to Wade and Chris, my sons, who willingly left all the things in America that make life seem so easy to a teenager. Making this move during your teen years required sacrifice. Thank you for being a special and important part of both life and ministry. You have brought me endless joy and much laughter.

Several women took the time to give preliminary edits to my book. You know who you are. Thank you so much for reading my early ramblings.

I am deeply grateful to Margaret Locklair for her tireless work on editing my book. She did a marvelous job of making corrections without compromising the way I speak or changing my story in any way.

Finally, I want to thank all of our prayer and financial supporters. Some of you have supported us since we first started in missions in 1987. Many of you prayed and still pray faithfully for us. Your letters to us on the field were always a great source of encouragement. Any "success" in the ministry is yours, as well, because of your co-laboring with us all these years. (Email: daybreak@sc.rr.com)

Introduction

I wrote this book at the urging of several women who had heard parts of my "outhouse" story. Knowing that some of my readers will have backgrounds similar to mine, I want the readers to know that God delights to use all of us in ways that glorify Him. If this book encourages at least one person to seek the Lord's will about entering the mission field or if it pricks one person's heart to support those on the field – all that I lived and experienced in this story will have been worthwhile. I hope, too, this book will encourage those who may feel that they have no call or purpose in life. I started my Christian life thinking the same thing and have no doubt now that God desires to use each one of us in the unique way He designed us. If exposing my own weaknesses helps a reader to see God's might used through our obedient, although sometimes weak, faith, I would love to hear from you and will rejoice with you!

I wrote primarily about the first year of our three-and-a-half year experience in Papua New Guinea, not because nothing significant happened in the last two and a half years, but because the deep lessons I learned from God during my first year were what sustained and encouraged me for the remainder of our ministry.

Many of the descriptions contained in this book portray my selfish focus on my own abilities rather than on God and His unlimited power. I fully relate to Peter when he asked Jesus to help him walk on water. When Peter took his eyes off Jesus, he began to sink. At points in my book I refer to this loss of focus as "splish splash."

All Scripture has been taken from the King James Bible and noted (KJV).

THE OUTHOUSE AT THE END OF THE EARTH

1

On the Mountaintop

I stood with slumped shoulders on a beautiful, small mountaintop, trying to keep the tears from flowing down my face. Sighing deeply instead, I stared glumly at the scene below where an outhouse was precariously perched on the side of the mountain. It was April 1990.

Many churches and individuals had prayed and donated money for my family to get to Papua New Guinea (PNG). I'd been in the country only two months. This was supposed to be my "mountaintop" experience, but I was miserable. I couldn't begin to imagine how I would survive. I wondered why I was even here.

I hated the outhouse! I blamed it for the way I felt and the problems I was facing. Not only did I hate the outhouse, I was terrified of it. Why in the world had God put me in a situation I could never be expected to handle? I'd like to say that, at that miserable moment in my life, I turned instinctively to God. But I was angry at Him for making what I considered a terrible mistake in sending me here – especially to a village so far from any semblance of civilization. I stared out at the lush, green mountains surrounding us, the very same mountains that I thought so gorgeous when we first flew over them. Now they seemed to be the cause of my isolation, hemming me in. I was despondent, even beginning to show anger toward my wonderful husband Bill, and I deeply resented the Lord for putting me in this situation.

How had I become this miserable woman in such a beautiful place? For several years I had prayed and struggled about coming to the mission field and had finally felt that God was calling me, as well as Bill, to serve here. I can remember so much of that process as if it were yesterday.

2

Our Family's Call

In 1985, I felt very satisfied with my life. I had become a Christian in 1978 and had been growing steadily in faith. In 1984, I left a demanding, full-time job as an accounting assistant in a large, multi-million dollar company to devote more time to my family. I worked part time as a secretary in our home church, Surfside Presbyterian, and loved every minute of it. I felt I was being effectively used by God. Bill had retired from the Air Force where he worked on aircraft radar systems and later as a manager organizing the training on the base. Now he was working for a local concrete company as an office manager. We were two ordinary people who had just finished our first careers. We were both heavily involved in various ministries, happy to be serving alongside many of our dearest friends.

Our pastor at the time, the Rev. Michael Ross, always spoke of the fact that, one day, God would begin to call people out of our young church, established in the early 1980's. As I listened to him, I thought how special it would be when God began using various people from our congregation in ministries outside the church to further His kingdom.

Never once did it enter my mind that our very own family would be the first one that God would call from our church. In fact, if you had asked me who was the most *unlikely* candidate for the mission field, I would have easily said it was myself. Even though I had moved around a lot as a child and a young adult, I was very much a city girl and not into any kind of risk-taking. I like running water, flushing toilets, air conditioning and being surrounded by all of my family.

My world began to turn upside down in 1985 after a mission conference. It was the first conference I had ever participated in, and it turned out to be the catalyst that thrust us into missions work. During the conference, we invited a missionary family to stay in our home. We enjoyed hearing of their successes and struggles. Bill, in particular, spent a lot of time talking with them and asking questions. I could tell he was enthralled by their stories about what God was doing around the world to save people's souls. After the conference was over, we decided to join the missions committee. I genuinely enjoyed being part of that committee and took the responsibilities seriously as our church learned how to minister to the missionaries that we supported.

Shortly after that conference, Bill came to me to talk over his feelings. He explained that he felt God was calling him to serve on the mission field. He told me a story from his impressionable childhood about visiting the neighborhood church and listening to stories about missionaries. He also reminded me about an encounter that haunted him – of a monk who approached Bill to talk about his Buddhist faith but refused to let Bill share Christ with him. It was then that the seeds were planted and Bill began thinking about how fulfilling it would be to become a missionary.

As he shared all of this with me, I realized that Bill was feeling called to foreign missions, a calling that I definitely did not desire nor share. We had recently purchased our first home. It was a brand new brick house in a new subdivision. Because all the houses were new, our neighbors had all moved into their houses around the same time and started to plant grass and trees and relationships. My sons had made friends.

I loved my house and my neighbors and saw our new neighborhood as a mission field in itself. In fact, in the few years that we lived there, we were able to pray with several of our neighbors to receive Christ. I could envision myself spending many years in that house, participating in the mission field right on our doorstep.

3

My Concerns

I never told Bill outright that I wouldn't go to the foreign mission field, although I was thinking it in my heart. God knew that I was digging in my heels. I listened politely to Bill and told him that maybe we could do something like that some day. After a while, he stopped talking about it. About a year later, we had another mission conference, and another missionary family, the Powlisons, came to stay in our home.

Keith and Ruth Powlison serve with Mission to the World, the sending agency for the Presbyterian Church in America, and had been called to Quito, Ecuador. Keith is a third-generation missionary and was fully able to address the fears that I had about taking two of our sons to a foreign country.

In talking to Ruth recently, she laughed as she remembered my saying to her earlier, "I guess if you can make it on the mission field, anyone can!" I honestly don't remember saying that to her, but as I think back on it now, I must have been wondering about my own ability to make it as a missionary.

I know we spent several hours talking to the Powlisons during their visit. After they left, Bill and I spent some more time praying and talking about how to know God's will for us, and I agreed to keep it a matter of prayer.

I have to admit that there were several issues in my heart that convinced me I would never go to the mission field. I thought about how much I liked the conveniences of "civilized" life. I had no desire to visit, much less live in, any kind of remote location. I also thought that Bill would "get over" this emotional reaction to yet another conference.

As I pondered and prayed over this some more, I imagined that if I ever did make it to a foreign field, it wouldn't be to an isolated area, but rather to a city, as it was for the Powlisons. Maybe then I could handle it! Notice here I say that *I* could handle it! That should let you into the secret places of my heart and reveal how little I was depending on God to direct me.

As I continued with this line of thinking, I decided that the best thing I could do was to become more heavily involved in the missions committee and the support of missionaries. Looking back, I believe I was bargaining with the Lord. I was assuming that if I did all of these things, He wouldn't send me away. I was acting as if the Lord couldn't possibly take care of me on the mission field.

Another big obstacle was our children. Two of our sons Wade, 13, and Chris, 12 were almost in high school. We also had Bill's four sons – Bobby, Brian, Scott, and Chad – that we would have to leave behind. Two of them were grown and two lived with their mother in England. How could uprooting two and being so far away from four be good for our family?

While I was worrying about our sons, Wade and Chris came to Bill and me at different times, privately, to tell us that they felt God was calling *them* into the mission field! Neither knew that the other had come to us, nor did they know that Bill and I were praying about this for our own lives. God was already starting to show me how fully He was in control. He was also showing all of us that He calls a family, not just the husband or the wife.

Sometime thereafter, I agreed that we could begin the process of applying to the various mission fields. I was still naively thinking that we would end up in a city, maybe in Europe, in some kind of support ministry. It's a good thing I had no idea that I would end up on that mountain top in Kungabip, probably one of the most remote spots in the entire world!

4

Moving Ahead

We filled out several applications with various mission organizations as we sought to know where the Lord would lead. It didn't take us long to realize that He appeared to be leading us to Wycliffe Bible Translators. We knew Wycliffe's reputation as an excellent, godly organization. We felt that we would benefit from and enjoy working with them.

One Sunday night, Bill asked for prayer at a Sunday evening service. He told the congregation that we were feeling God's call to the mission field and that we needed to know God's will. Interestingly enough, the very next week Bill was laid off from his job at the concrete company! I was making only a minimal salary from my part-time job and now Bill had no income. What in the world was the Lord thinking?

We approached some members of the missions committee at our church to ask if they would pray with and for us and to see if they sensed that we were, indeed, being obedient to follow God's will by applying to Wycliffe. They encouraged us to continue to apply and see how God would lead us.

We requested the paperwork to begin the application process. If you have never sought to join a mission organization, let me warn you – there is always a tremendous amount of paperwork to complete, forms to fill out, and references to obtain. I really didn't think we would be accepted. Bill and I had both been divorced, and I felt, and maybe hoped, that we would be refused for that reason.

However, we received news in the mail that we had indeed been accepted to attend Wycliffe's next Quest session in February 1987. This would be a five-week assessment time – for both Wycliffe and us – to see if we could minister together. Most people couldn't take off for five weeks to attend an assessment like that – but God had providentially provided us plenty of time since Bill was now working only occasional temporary jobs.

Through the church, we raised the funds we needed for the Quest program, obtained permission from the schools for our boys to be away, and packed up the car. We were off before I had much time to dwell on what was happening.

The Quest program, located at the JAARS (Jungle Aviation and Radio Service) Center near Waxhaw, NC, was challenging. Each family was under a microscope at all times, and we could feel it. The

20

staff was wonderful and loving, but we always had the sense that we were being scrutinized. We were grateful that we were able to get involved with a local church just across the border in Van Wyck, SC almost right away. Quite a few missionaries attended Trinity PCA because of its proximity to the Wycliffe center. We got to know the pastor, Richard Holmes, because he visited the center often. Trinity eventually began participating in our ministry by supporting us financially and as of the writing of this book, still does. There is a funny story behind that.

After we had attended the church one Sunday, Pastor Holmes told us that he would like to visit us. We were staying in a small trailer at the Wycliffe center. We gave him directions and told him that it would be fine for him to visit. A few evenings later, after a snowstorm, we were all in various stages of getting ready for bed. I was in pajamas, Bill was changing and Wade was in his underwear when we heard a knock on the trailer door. Because Chris was the only one appropriately dressed, we sent him to answer the door. Unbeknownst to us, Chris opened the door, saw Pastor Holmes standing on the steps, signaled him to wait, and promptly closed the door. After the rest of us threw on some clothes, we realized that Chris was in the house but Pastor Holmes wasn't!

Bill quickly opened the door and invited Pastor Holmes in. Wade offered to take his coat, but Pastor

Holmes, still shivering, said he would keep it on. Of course, we explained why none of the rest of the family had come to the door and apologized profusely. Pastor Holmes was gracious but remained a little reserved at first. This later became a great joke among all of us. He told us shortly afterward that the church would be supporting us, then kiddingly added, "Perhaps now you can buy some clothes."

We enjoyed our time at Quest. We decided to spend our five weeks concentrating on learning through the experiences being offered and to stop worrying about the results and how things would turn out. Language learning skills, cultural adaptation, and linguistic transcription training, as well as testimonies from some who had been on different fields for many years, were all part of our program.

Our kids had their own sessions where they learned about many facets of life on the mission field that specifically pertained to young people. We not only felt the pressure of being evaluated by the mission agency, but we also had the responsibility to home school the boys to help them keep up with their studies. Their local Christian school back home was very accommodating in giving us assignments so our boys could stay on track.

In the midst of this busy schedule, Bill came to me one morning to say that he realized we had gotten so busy we had forgotten the most important thing we needed for our spiritual growth: consistent quiet times of reading God's Word and praying. Here we were considering going to the mission field and already in danger of getting little or no spiritual nourishment! Bill gathered us together as a family and told us that our quiet times with the Lord were the priority, not just something we should do if we had time. He told us that if giving up that time meant that we might not get all of our assignments done, it was okay, because we would have our priorities in order. I appreciated his wise counsel. This lesson would come back to us later, and it is one that we still remember today. It's so easy to lose sight of what is really important. God graciously allowed us to learn this lesson and still get through all of our studies.

One assignment in particular stretched me during Quest. Each person was given a schedule and told that at a certain time, he would share the testimony of how God had saved him and then called him to the mission field. I'm not sure why, but I've never felt totally comfortable speaking in public, and I got more and more nervous as the days went by. As I write this, I have to chuckle because missionaries are asked to speak all the time. In fact, during some of our furloughs I have often been asked to speak at women's retreats. Once I was even scheduled to speak at a retreat on the heels of Elizabeth Elliott. She is a tough act to follow, but God continues to refine me in this area.

After I got over my initial concern about speaking to the Quest group, I began to think about what I might say. Several had already shared their testimonies, and I realized that most of the missionary candidates under the microscope with us had been raised as Christians – some in missionary homes. My home life had been far from Christian. I hadn't accepted Christ until I was in my late 20's. Prior to my conversion, I had lived what I once proudly called a "cosmopolitan lifestyle."

As I continued to dwell on my turn coming up, I began to think that perhaps I could give a testimony that didn't expose too much of my sinful past – one that might fit in better with the other testimonies I was hearing. It took only a short time to realize that would be a lie. I knew that I would have to tell my story as I had lived it. Because my testimony was so different from those of the other candidates, I wondered how God could use someone with a non-Christian background like mine when it appeared that He was more interested in calling His servants from homes that had served Him and taught their children well. Much later, I realized that God used some of the very difficult aspects of my childhood to strengthen me, to assure me of His constant presence now in my life, and to use me to help others with similar backgrounds.

5

My Beginnings

As I prepared my testimony, God revealed how perfectly He had designed my life: the difficult things as well as the pleasant. I also began to realize that my testimony was unique; no one else shared exactly the same story and God could use it to encourage others.

My life started in Guam on November 3, 1949, just a few years after World War II was over. My mother and father had enjoyed a whirlwind courtship. They met in San Antonio, Texas. She was enamored of my father's debonair looks and charm. The Air Force uniform didn't hurt either. In 1947, they were married before they really took time to think about it. After my father was stationed in Guam, my mother was able to get a job that allowed her to join him. I was born in a Quonset hut during a terrible storm. Within months, my parents separated and eventually divorced. I saw my father only four or five times before he died when I was in my mid-30s.

My mother remarried when I was less than two years old and my new stepfather adopted me. I wasn't to learn that he was my stepfather until I accidentally uncovered some documents when I was 13 years old. My stepfather was an alcoholic and very abusive. For my own safety, I left home at the age of 16 and lived with a family in Illinois. The hardest part about leaving was leaving behind my five brothers and sisters: Mary, John, Kathleen, Bill, and Rob. Even though we are technically half-siblings, we never think about it like that. We feel related, through and through.

At 17, after graduating from high school, I returned to San Antonio, moved into an apartment with two other single girls and thus started my independent life, away from family life.

In 1969, when I was only 19, I got married and knew almost immediately that the marriage would be a struggle. My 21-year-old groom and I were both immature and selfish. Our marriage lasted only nine years but produced two of my greatest blessings, my sons, Wade and Chris. Between the sexual abuse I suffered as a child and my divorce, I felt like damaged goods.

God began to send Christians my way. I had never heard the gospel before and had no idea that Christ had died for my sins. In fact, I had never acknowledged that I was a sinner. I suffered from what I call the "martyr syndrome," convinced that everyone was out to hurt me, never taking responsibility for my own failures. Once I recognized this, and once I acknowledged that I was a sinner in need of God's grace, I eagerly embraced Christ as my Savior.

A few years later, in early 1983, I met Bill. Struggling after a failed marriage, he was raising his four sons. Although I was wary because of my previous marriage, there were several things that attracted me to Bill. His commitment to the Lord was easy to see and we had many things in common! He was earnest and sincere, and we fell rapidly in love. After much prayer and counseling, we got married on September 24, 1983. Our pictures show us smiling, surrounded by six boys.

In spite of how much God had blessed me, I still didn't feel capable of being of any service to Him. Now, at Quest, all of those emotions resurfaced as the date and time of sharing my testimony approached. Finally my moment came. I am grateful to say that, on that cold fall evening, I shared my life in a truthful way — even though mine was very different from the other testimonies. I shared it with tears, knowing that I couldn't tell any story other than my own. God was already breaking me and preparing me for some difficult times ahead. Many in the Quest group expressed how my testimony had touched them and challenged them. I believe the Lord taught all of us that it is not *our* testimony that we share, but **His**.

Finally, the five weeks of Quest were completed. We had had a great time – life-changing in many ways. It was a wonderful period of bonding with other families seeking God's will in the same way that we were.

Now it was time to be evaluated and to see if we had been accepted. The staff began to meet, and we all began to pray. Each family unit was called in to meet with the panel to hear its decision. Praise the Lord! The anticipation and anxiety was over: everyone in our Quest group had been approved.

I can't remember exactly how many families that included, perhaps about 15. We were told that in most Quest programs, there were some families who were not approved. I was grateful that we didn't have to see someone turned down. We had fallen in love with each family that participated.

Shortly after our acceptance, Rick Wacek, a representative from the Huntington Beach, CA, office came to talk to all of us about our finances. As we chatted, I thought about my experiences as a junior accountant and wondered if perhaps I could use that background in our work with Wycliffe. But, even then, I was still not feeling that God was calling me to the mission field. He was calling Bill. I would just be tagging along.

As Rick, a Wycliffe missionary and accountant, talked about the problems they were having with a new accounting system at their headquarters, I jokingly said, "Too bad you don't have the McCormack and Dodge system, because I know that system well." I had learned this software accounting package from the ground up and had done extensive training on it at the company I had worked for.

Rick stared at me for a minute and then went on to tell me Wycliffe had indeed purchased the McCormack and Dodge accounting package. The problem was that only one man at headquarters really knew the system. He had diabetes and was on dialysis quite frequently. It was important to Rick that others learn this system to lessen the pressure and dependence on one man, especially someone so sick.

I couldn't believe it! I mean, what were the chances of this happening? Had God prepared me through my business background for the work that He was calling me to? Was I so important to God that He would do such a thing? I have to admit that up to this point, I figured I had been accepted as one of God's children by the skin of my teeth and had never felt that God had singled me out for anything. I mistakenly believed that perhaps God merely "tolerated" me. This was to be another turning point in my Christian walk as I realized that God could use the secular things of the world and the weak things of the world –

like me – to accomplish His marvelous purposes. God wanted to use me! I began to realize that God could use me in this call to missions as well as Bill. He wasn't calling just one of us; He was calling the two of us to serve Him as one. Plus, He was calling our boys!

Even though I realized the power of God to work out my life, to prepare me in advance to serve Him in missions, I began to have doubts about how He would work out the details. I realized that Rick Wacek and the others who worked with McCormack and Dodge were based in California. Since we had been told that we would do our management training in Dallas, TX, I surmised that I wouldn't be able to help out after all. Perhaps I could offer phone support.

I imagine it is easy for the reader to see that I am a feminine version of Peter in a lot of ways, especially at the point when he was in a boat and looked out to see Jesus walking on water. Peter knew that he was witnessing a miracle and initially showed great faith when he asked the Lord to let him walk on water, too. He even began to take those first steps of faith on top of the water and then – splish splash! – down he went. However, in spite of being In the midst of this miracle, and in the midst of realizing what power Jesus had, Peter's faith weakened.

I was also in the midst of a miracle, but I wasn't really responding in faith even though God had done all but speak to me in the deep voice I had heard in some old Cecil B. DeMille movies. All I was hearing was the same "splish splash" Peter heard. How much more I had to learn about all that God would be doing for me and my family! I still deal with weak faith at times, but I'm grateful for all that God was getting ready to teach me, because my faith did begin to grow.

Now that we were approved by Wycliffe, we began to pray about whether we felt God was still leading us to accept the call. Both Bill and I voted to proceed. I was feeling all right about our progress until Bill started suggesting that he was feeling more and more drawn to Papua New Guinea.

I had to tell Bill I had never heard of the country of Papua New Guinea. Geography has never been a strong suit of mine, so I began to do some research on the country. I learned that Papua New Guinea is exactly half-way around the world from South Carolina. Then I read about newly discovered naked tribesmen who lived there, some of whom had eaten a fellow human being for dinner not too many years previously! This was Papua New Guinea? This is where my sweet husband wanted to take his wife and children? Had he lost his mind? Didn't Bill realize that I could never make it?

Again, my eyes weren't on God and what He could do but on what I thought I was capable of doing. I knew that Bill and I were heading toward a management role in the mission organization, and we had been assured by several friends and missionaries that the Wycliffe center in Papua New Guinea was a very comfortable place to live, with running water and electricity. That put my mind somewhat at ease. Maybe I could handle that. Maybe I would never have to face the men-eating tribesmen!

When I prayed about the idea of an assignment in Papua New Guinea, rather than asking God to help me do His will by filling me with all I needed, I selfishly prayed that God would send me to an "easy" place. Was I thinking that I wouldn't need God's power? About two weeks after our acceptance into Wycliffe, we received a call from Rick Wacek saying that he was setting up a conference call with several people at headquarters, including some department heads. We weren't really sure what the call was about but agreed to be home to accept it. That day, when the phone rang, I expected the callers to ask for Bill, but instead, they asked to speak directly to me and proceeded to tell me how much they needed me in Huntington Beach.

I carefully explained that Bill's training was scheduled to take place in Dallas, but my callers stated that they had gone all the way to the top of the organization to get approval to personalize Bill's training and offer it to him in California, while utilizing my skills with the accounting software package. What a sense of humor God has! Now, not only was God showing me that the call to the mission field was also for me, it was starting to look as if, rather than my following Bill in his ministry, Bill could be following me! How many more times would God have to pull me up and set me back on top of the water before I realized how awesome and almighty He is?

Bill and I talked about this at length. We talked with our sons, Wade and Chris, to see what they thought. We all felt that God was calling us to do this, to make this change to Huntington Beach, CA. We accepted the challenge and direction from God.

6

Wade Teaches Us About Faith

It was time to sell our house! This was the house I had originally pictured myself living in until I was old and gray! It was 1987 and a bad time to sell. In our subdivision alone, there were many houses on the market. We hadn't owned ours for long and had little equity in it. A member of our church, a realtor, offered to help us sell but warned us that finding a buyer would take a long time. We already knew that we couldn't afford to pay the mortgage once we started out with Wycliffe. Also, Wycliffe had a policy that we could carry no debts to the field. Fleurette Elliott, our realtor friend, set up the paperwork but discovered she was totally out of For Sale signs because so many homes were on the market and not selling. We listed the house on a Monday, but it was Wednesday before Fleurette came by with the signs.

Bill and I worked with the Evangelism Explosion group at the church, which met on Wednesday nights.

That night, we went to our meeting and asked our friends to pray for the house to sell quickly. When we got home, Wade proudly announced that we had sold our house! He said that he had been sitting on the front porch when a white car had slowly driven by. He sensed that the occupants were really looking appraisingly at the house. Then the car came around again very slowly. Wade asked the Lord to have the car come by one more time if the passengers were going to buy the house – and it did!

The sale was a done deal as far as Wade was concerned. Bill and I were much more skeptical, and worried about what might happen to Wade's faith if these weren't our buyers. The next morning, while Wade was in school, Fleurette called to say that some people were interested in looking at the house on Friday. I cautiously asked her if they drove a white car! She didn't know and seemed surprised that I would ask such a question. When the boys got home from school, we told them about Fleurette's call. Wade grinned and said, "I told you!" I, in my weak faith, said, "They are just coming to look at the house. We'll probably have quite a few people come to the house." He just smiled again. The couple came the next day -- in their white car – and took a quick look inside and outside the house. They never opened a closet door or a cupboard. After a short while they thanked us and left. We were sure now that they weren't the buyers Wade was expecting (splish splash!). That is, until Fleurette called that night to say that we had an offer!

Our house sold so quickly that a neighbor came over to our house to ask us angrily what we had done to sell it so fast. He felt that we were doing something underhanded. I honestly don't remember what we told him but still remember his astonished questions. The house had sold in less than a week to Bill and Rose Rogers. Another part of this miracle was that we had worried about leaving our neighborhood because we still had some neighbors we were witnessing to. It turned out that Bill and Rose were Christians. In fact, we mentioned our church to them. They eventually joined Surfside PCA and Bill became a deacon in the church. Isn't God marvelous? New missionaries would be in place in our house, and we could move on.

7

Training in California

We left for Huntington Beach that summer, raising some of the financial support we needed as we traveled across the United States. We had so little money that we camped across the States, often smelling of wood smoke and trying not to scratch our chigger bites as we spoke in churches. We had some interesting experiences along the way and met some wonderful people. When we arrived in Huntington Beach and got settled into our apartment, we found out that Bill was to have his management training while also managing the apartments that Wycliffe owned and rented to the missionaries. I was to work in accounting to train personnel and refine the accounting system. We ended up staying there an entire year while God continued to reveal His plan to us.

Our kids enjoyed the area, but we were often overwhelmed by the difference in the California lifestyle versus what we were used to in South Carolina. Getting to a grocery store always involved lots of traffic. In the area where we lived, all the homes were behind cement fences and iron bars. I still remember Chris telling us about an experience he had with the youth group from the church we attended in Huntington Beach. He had been assigned certain tasks, including helping someone carry groceries. I guess because the crime rate was high in that area, he couldn't convince anyone that he was trying to help – not steal groceries!

We enjoyed the mild weather and being closer to our oldest son, Bob, and his wife, Deb. Amber, our first grandchild, was born during our time there, and we had some sweet times with her. Little did we know that part of the sacrifice of being in missions would mean that we would see very little of any of our grandchildren born while we were overseas – Amber and Justin, Bob and Deb's children; Ashli and Alex, Scott and Jodi's children; Brittany and Dylan, Brian and Trish's children; and Caitlyn and Alana, Chad's children. We continued to seek God's will about where He would have us serve. Bill still felt that God was calling us to Papua New Guinea. I was still struggling in my faith and thinking that I would never survive there, even if the Wycliffe center were modernized! To top it off, near the end of our year in California, Bill confided that he was beginning to wonder if he really wanted to work in the management sector after all. He felt that he was being called to work more directly with the indigenous people. Even though, yes, there were indigenous people at the center, he felt that he wanted to work in a village setting.

A village setting! What would that mean? I had been depending on that civilized center I had heard so much about. I had seen some videos from the area Bill was talking about, and wood smoke and chiggers sounded like a pretty easy life compared to what I had learned about tribal living. BUT - something miraculous happened. I agreed! I didn't know how I would survive, or what I would end up doing, but I was sensing the same call. That had to be the Lord!

We settled into our lives in Huntington Beach. Both boys enjoyed their schools. They really enjoyed the youth group at the church we attended. I worked hard in the accounting department while I learned and taught. Even though we weren't going through the standard hoops for management trainees, we were learning a lot and enjoying ourselves at the same time. It was a privilege to work with the people at the Wycliffe headquarters.

8

A Pineapple Points the Way

Several months after we began our work and training, we attended a Wycliffe regional conference. I had the opportunity to attend more sessions than Bill did, because of several meetings he had to attend. During one of the breaks, when snacks were being served, I bit into a slice of pineapple which shot juice about two feet in front of me and onto a man standing nearby. I read his name tag and learned that I had just squirted Frank Mecklenburg and that he served in Papua New Guinea. I made a joke about how he must be accustomed to wearing pineapple, and Frank began to tell me about his ministry.

He and his wife Charlotte had been in Papua New Guinea for quite a few years, translating the Bible for one of the many language groups there, the Faiwol people. I told him that Bill and I weren't translators, but that we had been seeking God's wisdom in just what we could do that would allow us to use our management skills. I also shared with him Bill's vision of using those skills in a village setting.

Frank became so excited at that point that he asked me to try to get Bill out of his meeting. With great enthusiasm, he told me that he and Charlotte had helped the Faiwol people establish a few small businesses in order to subsidize the literacy work in their language group. He was looking for someone with management skills who might train the Faiwol to run their businesses more effectively. I went to send a message to Bill, and as soon as he was able, he joined us to talk with Frank. It seemed the Lord had put us into each other's paths for a specific reason.

The more we talked with Frank and eventually his wife, the more convinced we became that this might be the ministry for us. As we sought the advice of our leadership, they told us that we would have to finish up the management course, which we had almost done, and then attend at least one semester of linguistics courses at the Summer Institute of Linguistics (SIL) in Duncanville, TX, to get the basic literacy skills we would need.

I was only a high school graduate and couldn't imagine myself taking graduate level linguistics courses. I wondered if I would be able to pass courses so difficult, which included courses named phonetics and morphology. Maybe, I thought, this wouldn't work out for us because I would never be able to get through the curriculum (splish splash).

When I expressed my concern, I was told we would need these specific credentials to obtain proper work permits to enter the country and serve there. At the time, neither Bill nor I saw the reasoning behind having to take yet more months of training if we were going to be working in a business setting, but I do remember one Wycliffe manager prophetically saying to us, "I think you might be doing more literacy there than you realize."

9

The Texas Bicycle Accident

After completing our year in Huntington Beach, we left our new friends in the summer of 1989 and went to Duncanville, Texas, just southwest of Dallas. Going through yet another move was hard on our teenagers in many ways. After leaving their school in Myrtle Beach, SC, they had attended one year of school in California and now would attend the Texas schools for only one semester. We were always grateful that they had been a part of the decision to go into ministry – it helped to be in agreement – but we knew Wade and Chris were sacrificing a lot in their own lives. We also began to realize how difficult it would be to leave behind our other four sons and their families.

We took some time to apply to Mission to the World (MTW) – more paperwork and interviews! We appreciate Wycliffe Bible Translators but wanted to also come under our PCA denominational sending agency in a cooperative agreement.

We started our courses: Morphology, Phonetics, Management, and Literacy. They were demanding and challenging. It didn't take long to realize that we definitely wouldn't match up to being translators – we struggled through the few courses that we took!

One thing I loved about that part of Texas was the hills. Coming from Myrtle Beach and then living in Huntington Beach, we hadn't been around hills for awhile. I started riding my bike back and forth to classes in order to gain strength for Jungle Camp, which was looming upon our arrival in Papua New Guinea. Our goal was to go to PNG by early the following year. One nice fall afternoon, on October 19, 1989, I left class as usual on Wade's bicycle. Bill had brought the car to school for some reason – I can't remember why. I think he had some errands that he planned to run after class.

He passed by me in the car, honking and waving, at the base of what I called "Killer Hill." I called it that because this particular hill was huge! When I had started my training a few months earlier, I could make it only a quarter of the way up before having to walk the bike to the top. Going down, though, was always fun. I had only recently been able to get all the way to the top without stopping and was so proud of myself. There was a high school perched just before the crest of the hill. I always watched for it, because I knew then that I was almost at the top.

That afternoon, just as I was approaching the top of the hill, I heard screeching brakes behind me. I thought perhaps two cars were about to collide. I was actually riding off the pavement, on the side of the road, but quickly headed further off to the side when I heard the brakes. Then I felt the impact of a car hitting me from behind! I vividly remember flying through the air – not with the greatest of ease – and starting to tumble as I fell. I honestly felt that I was going to be with the Lord that day and remember saying to myself, "Oh, well." I also remember calling out the name of Jesus. I landed in a gully that ran along the side of the road, with my head on one side of the slope and my feet on the other.

I was still alive! Amazing! I touched myself in several places just to make sure and began to assess the damage. This was in the day before helmets became a fashion and safety statement. I didn't have one on. The weather the week before had still been hot enough to wear shorts. This week, however, it was cold, so I was wearing heavier clothing. I had my skirt, leggings underneath, gloves and a moderately heavy coat. I discovered later that these things, plus the excess weight I was carrying, may have saved my life. It was the only time I was grateful to be overweight! I could tell immediately that I had broken my right wrist because of the way it was twisted. Little else seemed to be wrong with me. I even tried to stand up but thought it might be smarter to just sit and wait for help to arrive.

Students and teachers came running out of the high school. Shortly afterwards an ambulance crew showed up and put me on a back brace with head blocks, in case I had head or spinal injuries. I never lost consciousness and remember giving out my phone number, asking one of the teachers to call Bill, but he hadn't reached home yet. In fact, our son Chris answered the phone and the caller decided not to alarm him by telling him what had happened. The EMT's wanted to load me into the ambulance and take me off to the hospital immediately, but I was very concerned about Bill knowing what had happened first. Since we were so new to the area, it wouldn't be easy for him to figure out where the hospital was. I begged the EMT's to call Bill again. This was before cell phones, and the crew told me that they would wait only a few more minutes before transporting me to the hospital.

This time they did reach Bill, and he arrived just as I was being loaded into the ambulance. He followed us to the hospital, where I found out I had indeed broken my wrist – in fact it was somewhat shattered and required a pin to hold things together. I had sprained my neck and both of my shoulders. I also had sustained some impact on my stomach and the back of my legs. It ended up being a painful recovery, but I was so grateful to be alive!

My greatest concern was what this would do to our family's ability to attend Jungle Camp, which was due to begin in January. That gave me only eight weeks to recover. Meanwhile, I didn't know how I could possibly keep up with my classes (splish splash), but I had some wonderful instructors. Several came and personally tutored me and kept me on schedule with the assignments. Not only did I finish the courses, I made excellent grades. Bill still likes to tease me that I got the grades out of pity from the instructors who sat at my bedside and coached me. He might have a point there! I was just grateful to keep up! In the meantime, we wrote the director of Jungle Camp expressing our concerns about my ability to take part, especially in the physical portion. They replied that they were willing to work with me, so we proceeded with our plans, finished up our classes, and drove just ahead of an ice storm to get to Myrtle Beach, SC, in time for Christmas.

Shortly after arriving, Chris showed us several boils that had erupted on his body. This concerned us because while we were living in California, Wade had turned up with a bad boil on one of his knees. Wade's boil was very deep and developed into a serious staph infection, so serious that he was admitted to the hospital for several days to make sure it didn't go into his knee or leg bones. He ended up being fine. Chris had also developed several boils at different times. We were able to clear them up but a few more came up after we arrived in Duncanville. Eventually they seemed to come less frequently.

Now in Myrtle Beach, just a month shy of heading to Papua New Guinea, Chris had boils again! Right away, we took him to a doctor, who contacted the infectious disease specialists in Atlanta. They recommended that the whole family take a very strong antibiotic, because one of us might be a carrier of the bacterial culprit. We questioned the doctor, asking if we were wise to still try to go overseas when this was going on. He felt that we were on the right track. We all took the antibiotic, completing the course just days before leaving the country. The funny thing was that this particular antibiotic caused our body fluids to turn orange, so in the midst of all the goodbyes, our tears were a strange orange color.

10

From a White Christmas to White Sands

Arriving in Myrtle Beach before the winter storm hit was another example to us of how God protects us. It began to snow on Christmas Eve. Usually, if the beach gets any snow at all, it's a light dusting, but this year things were different. It was the first white Christmas in Myrtle Beach in 95 years! We ended up with almost two feet of snow. My sisters, who live in Florida, came up to spend the holiday with us. They arrived the day after Christmas because the storm extended all the way into Florida. What a beautiful way to celebrate our last Christmas in the States – snowbound and having great fun making snowmen and snow angels together.

After our special Christmas and some time of rest, we were ready to leave Myrtle Beach. We flew out very early the morning of January 25, 1990. I still had trouble walking because of the injuries to the backs of my legs where the car hit me, and I still wore a temporary cast on my wrist. Nevertheless, we were off. We flew first to California to attend the wedding of our son Scott to Jodi on the 26th. We then traveled from there to Huntington Beach, CA with our son Bobby, his wife, Deb, and Amber. After some tearful goodbyes, we flew out of California on January 31 and had a brief stop in Hawaii, staying with some friends there, Glen and Marsha Baugher. This couple had been members of our church in Surfside Beach and was now stationed at Hawaii's Hickham Air Force Base. They were to be supporters of ours for years as we served the Lord first in Papua New Guinea and later in Belize. Several things happened in the 36 hours we were in Hawaii that were not so funny at the time, but seem very funny now!

We had a ton of luggage with us. We were each allowed two 60 pound bags, and we had filled them to the maximum. That meant eight heavy bags to check, plus carry-on bags. In Hawaii, Bill began to complain about his arms, and we finally figured out that he had probably pulled some ligaments lugging those bags around.

Since we would be in Hawaii only one full day, we decided to see as much as we could, including snorkeling in the beautiful coral formations. Bill had decided to go barefooted as we usually do at Myrtle Beach and ended up with terrible blisters on the bottoms of both feet from the hot sand. He also was suffering from cramps and diarrhea. I can tease Bill now as I think back to how I thought I would be the one falling apart physically! I was doing just fine. My Scripture reading for the day was 1 Cor. 2:5: "Your faith should not stand in the wisdom of men, but in the power of God." (KJV) What a nice reminder of God's power being so much more dependable than my own abilities.

We left the next day, February 2, a little late because of mechanical problems with the plane. As we took off, an announcement came over the intercom that we had a very heavy load of baggage which might slow us down some (could they be talking about our bags?). The flight to Papua New Guinea is a long one. On this particular leg of the trip, the route would take us from Hawaii to Guam and then to PNG, all of which usually took about 14 hours. A few hours into our flight, the pilot came over the intercom again to repeat that we had an unusually heavy baggage load (us again?) and we were going into head winds, which meant that he would run out of fuel faster than anticipated. He went on to say that, as a result, we were going to have to make an unscheduled stop on an atoll called Majuro. An atoll is made up of a coral reef, which looks like a partially submerged doughnut with a shallow lagoon in the center. I had never heard of Majuro but Bill thought he remembered it as an important atoll during World War II. Later, my research revealed that all of the

Marshall Islands, of which Majuro is a part, were under Japanese control at one time.

Majuro has only one main road which runs 30 miles from the airport at one end of the portion of the island above sea level to the other end. The island is merely a half mile wide at the widest point. Even though some of the atoll was not above sea level, we could see the entire shape of it as we came in to land. It was truly an astonishing sight.

It was such a tiny island – hardly wide enough for our plane when we landed. As we looked out the windows, we could see the lagoon on one side and the Pacific waves lapping the shore on the other. Many of the residents of the atoll drove or bicycled out to see our plane. I imagine that they were as amazed about our being there as we were. There was even a fire truck standing guard.

Unfortunately, we weren't allowed off the plane during this unscheduled stop. We were told we were quarantined, so we sat back and watched the refueling through the windows. When we took off, the pilot asked us to pray and hang on because we were so heavily loaded (there it was again!) and the runway at Majuro was shorter than they usually required for a plane as large as this one. He also informed us that he had been told ours was the largest plane to land on this atoll since World War II. We got off again with no problems – thank the Lord!

This created a change in plans concerning the landing time in Guam. Because I was born in Guam, I was excited to have a four-to-five-hour layover there. I was just a year old when my mother and I left Guam and I knew it only by a few pictures I had. While we were there, I planned to take some time to take a taxi ride around the island. Unfortunately, our stop in Majuro had delayed us by about five hours, so it was very dark when we landed, and the connecting flight was already waiting for us. We were whisked from one gate to the other, loaded on to the plane and jetted down the runway! I never saw Guam.

We arrived in Port Moresby, the capitol city of Papua New Guinea, at 5:30 a.m. U.S. time, and I can't even tell from my journal what the date was!!! We had traveled for about 20 hours and crossed the International Date Line. Several of us on the flight were headed to Jungle Camp. We all climbed into vans which took us to the Mapang guest house and went straight to bed. The heat and humidity were unbelievable! Our sheets felt wet beneath us. I learned later that nothing ever feels totally dry in Papua New Guinea.

We woke up at 4:30 a.m. PNG time, our body-clocks adjusting to the 14-hour time difference between the east coast of the U.S. and PNG. We didn't really know what time it was for the first few days; we just got up when the sun did. It rained a lot, which made us feel wet and sticky. The realization was hitting me – we were in Papua New Guinea, a country few get to see and many have no interest in seeing. PNG is known as a backward country deeply affected by World War II. Later we would hear from some friends who had served in the armed forces there. One man in particular, who had been a pilot in the war, asked us if there were still cannibals! I never answered him because I didn't want to know the answer myself.

On our first full day, I was anxious to see the sights and experience the country. We soon got our chance when we left after a quick breakfast for a flight that would take us closer to where we would spend the next three-and-a-half months in Jungle Camp. The atmosphere at the airport was enough to send us spiraling right into culture shock. The terminal was filled wall to wall with people. Bill asked me and the boys to stay toward the back with our huge mound of luggage while he worked to get through the crowd. A few moments later I spotted Bill, standing way in the front, frantically signaling us. He motioned that the people at the ticket counter wanted our luggage – all of it!

Others around us, sensing our predicament, began grabbing our luggage as I watched with great concern. We had been warned to keep an eye on our belongings because of the frequent robberies in some parts of the country. The luggage was passed towards the front, hand over hand, above the line of people until it all got up front. So far I had seen no evidence of anyone trying to rob us or harm us – these people had just been gracious enough to save us a lot of trouble! We noticed that they handled the bags as if they weighed five pounds each instead of 60.

11

Learning Not To Be So Judgmental

We flew from the Port Moresby airport to the Madang airport. Our Jungle Camp directors, Jacque and Jaqueline Van Kleef, met us and gave us a short tour around town before we had lunch. Several other Jungle Campers had arrived and joined our group. We and our luggage all rode in the back of an open truck up the steep, winding mountain to Nobanob. A fellow newcomer screamed her way up some of the more precarious parts of the mountain. I was concerned about her fear and made an immediate judgment of her, thinking that she would probably never make it through the first week of Jungle Camp, much less the following weeks. My judgment of her was very wrong. She ended up being a courageous and gifted missionary who, along with her husband and family, is still serving in Papua New Guinea as I write this book.

After the scary ride up the winding mountain, we arrived in Nobanob, which would be our home for two-and-a-half months. We tried to come with open minds, but privately, I still wondered how I would ever survive. Because Bill and I were the only couple with teenage sons, we were offered a choice of where we would like to stay – either in a house up the hill or in a building that resembled old army barracks. We chose the house, which looked nice to us. It had electricity, indoor plumbing and even two bedrooms! How wonderful the Lord was, right from the start, to allow us and the boys some privacy. There were appliances in the kitchen because the house was normally inhabited by the staff. We were told that our meals would be prepared and served in the main area mess hall and that we could not use the appliances in the house. We promised that we wouldn't do so.

We went back to the main camp area, gathered up our stuff, and set off up the hill. We met some friendly and curious people as we walked by. It was kind of nice to spend the rest of the afternoon cleaning and organizing. We were all quite pleased with the results.

We had been told to bring mosquito nets and I quickly realized that the nets offered me protection from more than just mosquitoes. I always felt safer sleeping under the net: it kept critters from walking about my face and body. We would take the time to tuck the ends of the mosquito net under the mattress just as the sun started going down, making sure we weren't trapping any unwanted guests inside. At bedtime, I would lift up one small corner, crawl underneath and feel safe and snug for the night.

We quickly fell into the Jungle Camp routine. Classes in the morning covered topics ranging from survival skills to local culture. We sometimes hiked in the afternoon to build physical endurance. Nobanob was hot, like Madang, but a little higher because it was up a small mountain. Fortunately this meant that we would often feel the breeze.

About two weeks after we got there, we were told that we needed to learn to build a mud oven, constructed solely of mud, rocks and bamboo. We fashioned some of the mud so that it resembled a cat, using small bamboo pieces for the eyes, mouth, and whiskers. During the week we ate in the dining room, but on the weekends we would have to cook all of our own food in our mud oven, so we began to practice making bread in it. Cooking in the mud oven took much longer than in a conventional oven, but we ended up with edible bread, and it didn't taste bad. We found a piece of metal that we fashioned into a griddle and cooked several items on it, even making pancakes. We began to look forward to the weekends and being able to cook again in our little "cat" oven.

During the two-and-a-half months that we were at Nobanob, we "campers" made a few trips together as a group. Going down and eventually back up the mountain became second nature to us – even crossing one particular cement bridge that was in terrible shape. Because of the danger of collapse, everyone but the driver had to get out of the truck as it crossed. Yet, in spite of the bridge, it always felt good to get away. Our directors didn't have a problem with our going to town on the weekends on our own. They felt that getting ourselves to town and back was good training in how to get around in the country. Right now, a family outing sounded like heaven to us, so a few weeks into our stay, we decided to go into town. We had no transportation so we set off walking. Looking back on it, I guess we were pretty desperate.

We walked down the mountain and on into town. The one way trip was about two miles. Even that didn't dampen our determination to get there! In town, we enjoyed seeing all the sights. The park was very unusual because of the thousands of bats hanging from trees right in the middle of the town. They made a terrible racket and a terrible smell – almost like rotting meat. In fact, the smells in the town were different from any I had ever experienced. Some of the good smells emanated from flowers, the salt air, and the different cooked foods being sold by vendors. Some not-so-good smells were from mildew, urine on the side streets and rotted foods left on the side of the road.

Nevertheless, we were delighted to be in a different environment and continued on, happily "window shopping." The day we spent in town was a gift to us. It helped us feel as if we had a little freedom. We were also able to buy some groceries for the weekend, including some canned, processed meat that we hoped we could prepare with pancakes. We hardly ever eat canned meat now, but it seemed as precious to us then as a filet mignon.

The time came to head back to camp. We made the trip to the base of the mountain with no problem, but by the time we were about halfway up, we were extremely hot and tired. The narrow, winding road going up the mountain was in open sun and we didn't have enough water with us. Right about the time I was thinking I couldn't take another step, a pickup truck stopped and offered us a ride. All of us eagerly accepted and jumped into the truck bed. We did become a little concerned when we noticed that the fellows sitting with us were wearing beer can pull tabs bent over their earlobes as earrings!!! Thankfully we got back safely ... and on time.

One family got to Jungle Camp about a week later than the rest of us because of some problems they had with their visas. When this family of four showed up, the boy and the girl were both wearing Mickey Mouse ears that they had gotten in Disneyland. The mother was wearing tons of makeup, which was running profusely down her face. They looked totally out of place to us, and we stared at them as if they were from Mars. I guess we thought we were accomplished bush people by then. This Disney group ended up being a great family, but I'll never forget my first wrong impressions of them.

I realize how often I jump to conclusions upon meeting new people. How quick I am to form opinions based on what I see or hear from them – whether someone is screaming on the way up the mountain or arriving at Jungle Camp wearing makeup and mouse ears. How, I wonder, do we look to God at times? He doesn't look at the outward appearance of a man, but at the inward appearance. This makes me humble and repentant as I ask the Lord to help me see people with His eyes. I can only imagine what people thought when they saw me arriving at Jungle Camp, overweight and limping from my biking accident.

One physical challenge that awaited us was the one-mile swim that we would eventually have to accomplish in the ocean. The thought of this was daunting enough to me, but I was to discover that several people in our group couldn't swim at all. We made several trips to Nagada to prepare for our swim. From our Jungle Camp site on top of the mountain, we could see Nagada and the beautiful water far below. The water in this lagoon was made up of about thirty shades of blue filled with the most beautiful coral in the world, not to mention hundreds of varieties of tropical fish.

We were required to meet certain swimming goals each time we went. Once we met our goal for that particular trip, we were free to swim and snorkel at will. It was a wonderful experience. All sorts of poisonous things lived in the water – scorpion fish and sea snakes, to name a few – but we blissfully swam, being careful not to step on anything that might hurt us. The staff members were a great witness to me as they worked patiently with the non-swimmers. Some of them eventually swam a mile. All four in our family met our goal to swim a mile – something I thought I wouldn't be able to do, especially still healing from the accident. I think now that the salt water and physical exercise actually aided my recovery.

One day, one of us spotted a lobster! We had been living off a variety of foods unusual for Americans and were pretty tired of some of it. The lobster was a blessed sight. Several of us tried to corner him, imagining how he would look on our dinner plate that night. Unfortunately for us and fortunately for him, the lobster was much quicker than we were and disappeared into the sea. We were destined to have more of our canned mackerel, after all.

Wade had an interesting experience one afternoon while swimming. A remora (a fish that likes to attach itself to sharks) seemed to be without a shark partner and was determined to hang on to Wade. Wade would swim away and the remora would come for him. He finally had to get out of the water to escape it.

12

Stepping on a Death Adder

About three weeks into Jungle Camp, there was a special night designated to prepare dinner for our "was-family," the Papua New Guinea family who had adopted us during our stay. All four members of our was-family were friendly and talkative. They were older, like we were, with two teenage sons. We had already enjoyed a few visits together and were excited about the opportunity to have them at our "place" and to be able to serve them a meal.

I worked hard on the dinner. Cooking over an open fire and in a mud oven didn't come naturally to me. I wanted everything to be perfect and was proud of the meal that I had prepared. We had electricity, but to create what I thought would be the perfect mood, I had turned the lights off and had only the oil lanterns burning for light. Things seldom happen on time in third world countries, and Papua New Guinea is no exception. Our was-family arrived about an hour and a half late. I actually wasn't too upset about that and had managed somehow to keep things warm. I was certainly glad to hear their voices coming down the path, though, as we had gotten pretty hungry. Bill, the kids and I walked to the door to greet our guests. As I took my last steps to the door, I stepped on something like a rope. Then I realized that the "rope" was wriggling under my foot. I jumped back, screamed, and flipped on the lights. The "rope" was actually a small snake.

Wade was able to corner the snake and get it into a jar. Later, when he showed it to the staff, we found out that I had stepped on a death adder! Apparently I scared him as much as he scared me, and he wasn't quick enough to bite me. Once things settled down, we started to turn the lights off again, but our was-family solemnly and firmly instructed us to leave them on. I think they had a healthy respect for this very venomous snake, too. I don't remember what we ate that night, but do remember that we talked well into the night, telling each other about our families and memorable life experiences.

13

Campfire Building at its Worst

One thing I appreciate about the Papua New Guineans is the importance they place on relationships. As an American, I'm often way too goal-oriented. As I visit with someone, I usually have an agenda in mind and a goal to reach. The New Guineans aren't like that at all. Their goal is to spend time building their relationships, usually with little or no agenda. The lessons I learned from them have helped me greatly, even in Belize, where we later served for nine years as missionaries.

We had quite a bit of homework throughout the Jungle Camp session. One of the exercises was to tell a story in Pidgin English (also called Tok Pisin or Neo Melanesian), using the words that we had learned. I thought I was learning the language pretty well and went to tell my story to one of the national people picked to hear it - my regular Pidgin English teacher. I launched into my story, really getting into the words I had learned, only to discover that my teacher couldn't follow me at all. I ended up having to read my story to him, instead. I was disappointed in my lack of progress.

Another challenge we faced in late February was to build a fire outside. We camped all the time in the States and had built quite a few fires. Bill was particularly good at fire-building, and I thought I was, too. Unfortunately, it had rained fairly heavily the night before our test, and had rained some more that morning. Bill set out to build the great fire that we were feeling confident about, sending me in search of firewood. I gathered what I thought were pretty good pieces for the fire.

My husband usually bends over backwards to compliment me and to be positive in the ways he talks to me, but I remember that whenever I brought him a piece of wood, he told me that it was either too wet, too small or too big. He was feeling the stress of not being able to start the fire and I was getting my feelings hurt as I tried to find the pieces that would do the trick. Even after my many forays into the bush to get the proper kind of firewood, we never really got a good fire going. I remember looking at the couple next to us, who had a huge bonfire going. It didn't help when Bill remarked how well they were building their fire. I began to think that I wasn't cut out for Papua New Guinea. I could neither speak the Pidgin English language nor build a fire (splish splash)!

14

When Falciparum Malaria Can Be a Good Thing

Our was-family didn't live very far from us, and we often hiked up to their place when we had free time. One day as we were talking with our papa, Begbeg, he began to tell us a story about his father, who had been a pastor of the church that we could still see on top of Nobanob. When the Japanese came to the village during World War II, they searched for all the pastors of churches and told them to burn their Bibles and any other religious materials. When our papa's father refused to burn the Bibles, he was killed and his corpse beheaded. Begbeg's story made us realize how deeply Papua New Guinea was affected by a war its people had never sought to participate in. Later, we would hear stories from our own village of Olsobip. As isolated as they were in these mountains, the people still had quite a few stories to tell of the World War II era.

In fact, we were in Olsobip the next year – 1991 – when the Gulf War broke out, and we witnessed the fearful reactions of the people. Some came to our house to ask Bill if the war would arrive in the village. They were concerned that the end of the world might be coming. Their questions gave us great opportunities to encourage them to share God's word. It also showed us the emotional scars the Papua New Guineans still carried from the last war.

One day, some of the men and teenage boys of Jungle Camp went on a long hike. Bill and Chris discovered parts of an old Japanese plane left from World War II and brought pieces back to show me and the others who didn't go on the hike. Bill brought back other souvenirs as well – we counted well over 130 mosquito bites on his body! He said he had encountered swarms of mosquitoes every time he stopped walking. It's a miracle that he never got malaria from that experience. Wade didn't go on that hike with Bill and Chris, but was to have a frightening experience with malaria a short time later that would test my faith and once again reveal God's perfect plan to me.

We were allowed to go down to Madang for an International Night that a Christian ship, the Doulos, was presenting. This ship travels around the world providing medical care, evangelizing where it docks. We were excited to have a chance to get away from the normal routine and join other believers in worship.

69

The boys had arrived a few hours ahead of us and were helping the crew set up for the worship service. Shortly after Bill and I got there, enjoying all the new sights and sounds, someone came running up to tell us that Wade was extremely sick.

As we hurriedly followed him, the messenger told us that Wade had gone with the band to help them set up their sound system when he started feeling sick. As he began to feel worse, Wade decided to lie down in a car. By the time we got there, he was almost unconscious. Anyone who has ever had a very ill child knows what I felt in the pit of my stomach. This was not something ordinary. We were told that we could take Wade onto the Doulos, which had a hospital and a medical staff. The Jungle Camp group was supposed to rendezvous at a certain time, and it looked as if we might miss the time, so it was important that someone notify the director and others what was going on. Frantically, we tried to locate someone. When we weren't able to, Bill decided to stay behind with Chris to make sure he was all right and to let the group know what was going on.

Two strong men carried Wade to the ship and up the dock. I could tell things were very serious and wondered if we had risked Wade's life or would lose him before our time in Papua New Guinea had really started. After running some tests, a very kind doctor from Romania diagnosed Wade with Falciparum Malaria. The doctor told me the bad news: this was the worst type of malaria to get. Wade was seriously ill. The doctor also told me the good news: this kind of malaria doesn't recur like other strains do.

During the night, Wade's temperature soared to 104, but by morning he was doing better after receiving the appropriate medicine. God was sparing my son – in fact, He had sent him a ship full of medical personnel – and I was so grateful. As I write this, I think about how God didn't spare His own son but sent Him to die for us – for me! How could He possibly love me that much? Wade was well enough to join the ship's team for lunch. We felt as if we were eating like kings in a palace. The food was plentiful and fresh! Much of our Jungle Camp experience was about teaching us how to survive with the provisions around us. Because of that, we had been living on canned mackerel, rice and very little fresh meat or produce other than certain fruits.

Wade and I laughingly commented that maybe we should change mission organizations! I remember being asked if we wanted seconds! I also remember mashed potatoes and brussel sprouts. I don't usually get all that excited about brussel sprouts, but having green vegetables excited me that day. Knowing how much Bill loves brussel sprouts, I managed to scrounge up a jar and took some back for him. He was delighted to have them, and once again we saw God displaying His goodness to us through a tough time – from a scary experience with malaria to brussel sprouts.

We were able to return to Nobanob the next day. Wade recovered fully and quickly. The doctor had been right when he said that Wade wouldn't have recurrences of the malaria. He never did. We were grateful for that because Jungle Camp was strenuous and stressful enough without being sick on top of it all.

15

Overnighting in the Bush

We stayed busy at Jungle Camp attending our classes and continuing to build our endurance by going on hikes. Sometimes the humidity and mosquitoes became unbearable. A note in my journal reminds me of just how humid it was. One day the moisture got to Wade's guitar – it came totally unglued. It made me pause to thank the Lord for the fact that our family was holding up better than the guitar!

Jungle Camp was slated to last for three-and-a-half months – two-and-a-half months at Nobanob with an additional five weeks of village living. The village living time loomed in front of us. Each family in our group would go off to live in a different village for a total of five weeks. I don't think any of us were looking forward to it. Most of the campers were going to villages they would never see again because they didn't have their assignments yet. Because we already knew which village we would be working in, we were given permission to spend our five weeks there. Frank Mecklenburg (the victim of my squirting pineapple) was making the arrangements, and the day came when we got a letter from him saying that we would be staying with a native couple and their eight children! I would like to be able to write here that I obediently went along with that plan and turned all of my concerns over to the Lord. What I did instead was to say that I wouldn't, under any circumstances, EVER make it if I had to live for five weeks with a Papua New Guinean family with eight children!

Bill agreed and we wrote to Frank asking if there were a house – any house – we could use to avoid staying with a family for so long. Frank wrote back to say he had found another house. We found out later it was a house the villagers were getting ready to burn down because it was so old, but they decided to keep it for us. Although the thought of a condemned hut in Papua New Guinea might not sound too appealing, having any place we could call our own "home" for five weeks sounded good to me. I didn't realize it then, but I can see now how much the Lord was changing me.

To train us for this village living experience, we were taken on an overnight adventure in the bush. We had already had several classes preparing us for this, including our memorable fire-building class.

We'd learned how to build beds and shelter in the bush and felt that the training we'd had cooking over fires and in mud ovens would also come in handy.

We were divided into three groups. Despite our ages, Bill and I were part of a group of mostly young families. The directors picked a site that would be relatively easy to reach, since I was still having problems with my legs. Our boys, however, opted to go off with the real "jungle" boys, the hardier group. So, Bill and I were like honeymooners, with no kids. All the other families with us had several small children. We got our bed and shelter constructed and even got a fire set up early. A friend of ours from the U.S. had mailed us marshmallows and we had smuggled them into camp. I say smuggled because we really weren't allowed to take any special foods with us. I had already collected the firewood (much drier and better this time) and stored it under the tarp.

It usually got dark around 6 p.m. every night of the year, because we lived so close to the equator. Bill and I felt that some of the other families could use some extra hands so we went around offering our help as they constructed their lean-tos. We learned later that some of the couples felt tremendous pressure to get several beds made plus a good structure erected before darkness fell.

Two of the staff, who had come to assess and protect us, stayed busy while everyone else worked on their structures. We wondered what they were doing and had a good laugh when we looked up to see that they had a constructed a "bus stop" bench and were lounging on it, reading a Time magazine and drinking Coke! What a funny contrast to what we were going through. We hadn't seen a Coke or a magazine for a month.

We gathered together at our fire and got ready to enjoy the "contraband" marshmallows. The two staffers were invited, of course. Then the Van Kleefs (the Jungle Camp directors) showed up at the site. Just as they were admiring our fire, one of the little girls came up to ask when we were going to roast the marshmallows. The Van Kleefs paused for a second or two and then asked if they were invited as well. We loved them even more at that moment. They were such good leaders, and they didn't seem to mind the smuggled marshmallows.

We all headed off to our new "lean-tos" and most of us were asleep by around 9 p.m. Bill had done a good job on our beds, though we still had trouble sleeping on small branches tied together. We did manage to stay dry and get some sleep in spite of the light rain that fell that night.

Some of the other groups didn't fare as well. A few, like our boys, were sleeping in hammocks, and got pretty wet. One family told the story of slowly losing all their kids during the night. It turns out that their beds were constructed on the slope of a hill, and, during the night, each child rolled off and into the brush. They did finally find all their kids. I still chuckle as I remember that night – who would've thought I would EVER do something so primitive? In my own power, it wasn't possible. I'm thankful that God enabled me to do what I did. I enjoy giving Him the glory.

16

You Dirty Rat!

We frequently heard rats scurrying around at night in our little house at Nobanob. I wasn't enjoying the sensation of thinking one might run across me while I was sleeping. Every night I made sure to sleep only under the mosquito net. One night, Bill got up in the middle of the night to use the bathroom and was stunned to see a rat swimming in the toilet. Apparently the rat had fallen in and couldn't get himself out. Bill took care of the rat by knocking him on the head and tossing him outside. Of course, all four of us had to squeeze into the tiny bathroom to see what was happening. Knowing the rat was gone made me feel safe enough to go back to sleep, but that sense of security was short-lived.

A few nights later, again in the middle of the night, we were awakened by small animal cries. Bill had to take a portion of our rattan wall apart to find a whole nest of baby rats. They were promptly moved out of the house, too! I realized my sense of security had to come from God, not my perception of the current rat population.

Between these two sleepless nights, we had an overnight stay with our was-family – part of the training that we had looked forward to, not stressful sounding at all. We liked this family very much and felt that we would have a great time with them. We weren't disappointed.

When we got to our was-family's house, we could see that they were scraping the insides of coconut halves with a special tool. They mixed water with the coconut shavings and squeezed the shavings with their hands to make a milk-like liquid. They then took the "milk" and added it to the rice they were cooking and tossed the squeezed coconut shavings to the ground for the pigs and chickens, which eagerly gobbled them up. When they served the rice to us and we tasted it, we found it wonderfully delicious!

The Papua New Guineans eat quite a bit of rice. It's one of their primary staples, even though the crop was introduced to the country. Other staples are indigenous, including taro, a root vegetable, and sago, which comes from the pulp of the sago palm. When we later had opportunities to visit other parts of the country, we could see that most areas used sago but sometimes prepared it in different ways. All started the process similarly, though – they would harvest the pulp from the sago palm, beat the pulp mixed with water and end up with a pasty treat, about the consistency of peanut butter, just not as tasty!

When we later arrived in Olsobip, one of the villages in our language group, we found that the Faiwol people also prepared sago this way, though in other areas, they would fry it up. I decided eventually that I liked the fried version better! Our was-family had rolled sago into some of the coconut that hadn't been used to produce the milk for the rice. We weren't usually all that fond of sago, but the coconut disguised, or should I say enhanced, its flavor.

We enjoyed sitting around the food and the fire and talking with our new family. It was fun to have time with them and to learn from them. Most Papua New Guineans would tell you that they didn't feel as smart as Americans, but it didn't take us long to realize how very smart they are.

The New Guineans go to bed fairly early because they get up so early. We went to bed when our was-family did, sleeping on the floor. We were awakened sometime in the middle of the night with the entire house swaying on its stilts. I remember thinking that, if the house fell down, at least it wouldn't have far to fall and there was very little stuff that could fall on us or hurt us. Once the shaking stopped, we stayed awake for awhile until we fell into a restless sleep. The next morning, when we asked our was-family about the earthquake which had awakened us, they stated that they had never even felt it!

17

Always Ask the Rental Agent If His Boat Leaks

There was never a dull moment in Jungle Camp. Shortly after our overnight adventure, we were asked to go to a different village to conduct a survey. The survey would assess how many people were in the village and how many were literate, among other interesting facts. The men went one way and the women the other. We women had to go by boat. We hired a nice fellow to help us cross, but we never thought to ask him how "sea-worthy" his boat was. It would have been a good question to ask because we had to help bail as we went along, wondering if we could keep up with the volume of water entering the boat through a good-sized crack in the bottom. For a while, the other women and I thought that we might have to put our mile-long swimming techniques to use, but we arrived on shore safely.

As we neared the village, we could see a man coming towards us. He stopped under a canopy of coconut trees and began to beat a drum. Did his rhythm mean something to the other listeners? We prayed that he was simply calling people from the village to come out to help. We were right. Several people came to us, mostly women and children. We felt welcomed and enjoyed our visit while gathering our information. It was a good way to practice my terrible Pidgin English.

18

Preparing for Village Living

Because Papua New Guinea sits so close to the equator, the climate in the lowlands is very hot. Consequently, we were almost always hot and sweaty. Wondering how hot it really was, we unpacked a thermometer we had brought with us. One day when we were miserable, Bill laid the thermometer on the grass, where the thermometer soon broke because of the high heat! We never bought a replacement nor did we ever try again to measure the temperature. We figured it was better not to know.

I made a strange notation in my journal on April 5th: "We had a lot of rain today and it got so cool that we put on sweats and sweaters!" I doubt that the temperature was really that low, but the difference was enough to make us feel cold. It was a wonderful feeling and special enough for me to make note of it. Maybe thermometers are overrated.

Being in Jungle Camp was often very stressful. I was still struggling with my disabilities from the bike accident and felt frustrated by the things that I couldn't do. The other missionaries had their struggles as well. One particular evening, a man in our group stood up to share a prayer request at the nightly meeting. His wife, he said, was having an anxiety attack about living in the village, particularly about the trial village living experience that was coming up. She had told him just that evening that she wouldn't go. He was in tears as he explained this. We spent quite a while praying for him. God answered our prayers. Not only did they go as a family to their trial experience, but his wife worked faithfully alongside him in their permanent village for several years. Obviously, many of our concerns resulted from not really knowing what to expect. As soon as he expressed himself so openly, I realized my own dark secret. I didn't want to go either – I was just not brave enough to tell Bill or the kids!

I continue to marvel at what the Lord does in us and through us as I see how many of my first impressions about people were wrong. There were some I thought would never make it who ended up being among the godliest and most productive people serving on the field. I'm sure it was because they had to depend more on the Lord than did those who felt so prepared. It would later give me much hope and encouragement to know that God wasn't relying on my talents but on His own marvelous works!

We had completed the first two-and-a-half months of Jungle Camp and we were scheduled to begin the next five-week segment, village living, on April 11. My primary emotion by then, surprisingly, was one of excitement and enthusiasm because we had waited so long for this experience – to finally meet the Faiwol people that we had heard so much about. My other emotions included fear of the unknown, fear of not being able to survive, and fear that something terrible might happen to us in such an isolated place. I realize now that all my fears were based on my perception of my own abilities (splish splash).

We were scheduled to fly into our village in a single engine Cessna and could carry only so much for the five weeks that we would be living there. We found out that we were over the weight limit, between our own personal weight and the weight of our baggage, and had to leave the majority of our food back in Madang. The pilot said that he would get it out to our village within a week! What? Wasn't it enough that God had brought me out to this remote village – would He expect me to suffer even more?

It seemed that the Lord was already starting to take familiar things away from me. I knew that we would need to learn to eat native foods in our village but had planned to supplement with a lot of American-style foods. We weren't quite sure how we would manage until the plane returned, but I finally decided that it would do me little good to worry about it.

The flight to our village was absolutely beautiful! Almost everything in Papua New Guinea is green. The trip provided us with a bird's-eye view of lush green mountains and some spectacular waterfalls. It took about one-and-a-half hours to get to Tari where we refueled. Refueling was an interesting process. Someone would roll out a drum of gas. To fill the plane the pilot had to stand on a ladder, holding the nozzle in one hand while someone else cranked the pump inside the drum. After our refueling we had another 50-minute flight, more or less, before we arrived in our village.

As we flew closer to Olsobip, we came in through a break in the mountains, crossing the Fly River, which was breathtaking! The river snaked its way through the mountain valleys and seemed to point the way to our village.

We were immediately surrounded by mountains on three sides, including one right in front of the spot where our plane made a quick touchdown. We made a slippery landing on the wet, grassy airstrip, ending our trip in what we later called a "fish bowl." Olsobip sat in the middle of the "bowl." Frank Mecklenburg told us sometime later about a couple of planes that didn't stop on time and ended up crashing into the mountain. It was good not to know about the crash on our first trip.

19

Adopted by the Shortest Family We Ever Met

A welcoming committee was waiting for us, probably 50 people, most of them smiling. A man about five feet tall came up to us immediately and identified himself as our "Papa." He told us that he had adopted us into the tribe, and introduced us to our "Mama," who was a little taller than he was. He proceeded to tell us how we were related to most of the people standing there at the airstrip. We hadn't been there five minutes and already had a mother, father, brothers, sisters, and lots of aunts, uncles, cousins and more. The Western Province, and particularly the Star Mountain area where we were, had been well known in the past for its cannibalism. It was encouraging to know that as "family," we would most likely not end up in anyone's soup pot!

The pilot told us that he would have to leave us immediately since the weather was starting to close in. Because of the "fish bowl," the weather usually settled into Olsobip every afternoon and the pilots didn't like to sit around long. As he got ready to taxi off, I reminded him that he was to come back and bring us our food in one week. Then the realization sank in – he was leaving us here! There was no way out! There weren't even any roads. Tears streamed down my cheeks as I watched him take off. I wonder what my new "family" thought of me.

You probably know me well enough by now to realize that I didn't turn immediately to the Lord at this point. I confess that my first thought was not of the Lord but of the fact that Frank had a radio that he was going to let us use, and that if we got into any trouble I could call someone and he would come and get us. It's a good thing I didn't know the Lord would take that away from me, too. A short time later, we found out we could hear over Frank's radio, but the microphone was broken and no one could hear us! When would I ever learn that it is the Lord I must turn to first? (splish splash.)

Daniel 4:22 comes to mind as I write this: "It is thou, O king, that art grown and become strong: for thy greatness is grown, and reacheth unto heaven, and thy dominion to the end of the earth." (KJV) It is so comforting to know that God is with us at all times and in all places. Even to the "end of the earth." I would need to rely on these verses many times.

After meeting our family and standing in the hot sun for a bit, we realized it was time to start the hike to our new home. In our ignorance we never thought to ask Frank how far we might have to hike. We naively assumed that we were heading toward a point at the base of the fish bowl. Unfortunately for us, not only were we not headed somewhere close by, but we were also going to climb one of the mountains forming the walls of the fish bowl. It isn't that the mountain was extremely high; it was just that we hadn't counted on it and were now standing at the bottom, fully loaded with our belongings but with no water. It was midday and extremely hot. No matter where we traveled after that day, we never again left without water.

Members of our new family quickly grabbed our belongings and we began the climb. I was so embarrassed by how many times I had to stop to catch my breath. These people were probably wondering if I would really make it to the top. Bill was faring better than I and the boys seemed okay. We eventually made it to the top, and as soon as we caught our breath, asked for some water to drink. We knew that whatever the people offered would have to be boiled for at least 20 to 30 minutes, but we were hoping that we could get a fire going and start right away.

Papa sent some young girls to get the water. They returned about 30 minutes later with sweat dripping from their brows. I wondered how far they had had to go and how we would get water later, on our own. I figured it was better not to know at this point, but knew it had to be distant to take them as long as it did. I had seen how quickly these people could move around. Since I hadn't seen anyone else sweating going up the mountain, I could only imagine how arduous their journey might have been. We were so grateful to see the bucket of water in the girls' hands. As the four of us looked into the bucket, we could see that the water was a light, yellowish color. The water could have been purple at that point and we would still have boiled it and drunk it.

Our fire-building practice came in handy as we began to build a fire so that we could disinfect the water. We were praying that we would have better success this time than on the trial run at the jungle camp training grounds. Even though the wood was wet we were able to get the fire going within an hour, find one of our pots and boil the water for the required time. When we finished, the water was, of course, extremely hot, but being so thirsty we blew on our cups and began to drink it – with grateful hearts. We overlooked the yellow color and a slight burning sensation, greedily drinking several cupfuls. No one else accepted our offer of water and I wondered why.

Now that we had had something to drink, we began to look more closely at our house. I remembered hearing that our papa had considered burning down our little house before we arrived because it was so old. It did look old and dried out compared to the other thatch houses. The house, like others around it, was raised three feet above the ground on stilts. The outside walls were made out of bush material held together by thin wood logs about two feet apart and the roof was corrugated tin. There were four rickety steps (no handrails, of course) that led us into the house. The entire house was only about 200 square feet (the size of a one-car garage). Most people might complain about this, but I don't remember any of us ever feeling cramped. Probably the fact that we didn't have a stick of furniture made it seem bigger!

Once inside we noticed the walls were woven from long, narrow leaves. The flooring was made from tree bark, and looked like bamboo. There were four small rooms – the main front room which served as a living room, two rooms we used as bedrooms, and a tiny closet-like space we eventually used as a shower room. We had brought air mattresses with us to serve as our beds. In the boy's room, Wade placed his air mattress on the floor and Chris set his on a wooden pallet that Bill had quickly built.

We continued to do some things around the house to get set up. There were still a lot of people standing around watching us. I'm sure we were more entertaining than TV – which they didn't have. When we walked outside again we noticed that there was a large rain tank right behind our house! We asked about it and learned that it had a leak and didn't hold water. Always the optimist, I mentally added to our "to do" list to get it fixed.

Some of the people began to help us construct a makeshift hauskuk (kitchen). The people built their kitchens as separate buildings because of the extreme heat and to protect their main house from burning down in case of a fire in the kitchen. Their hauskuks looked very much like smaller versions of their houses – bush material for the walls and roof. Ours, however, was more rustic. It consisted of six poles, three on each side, holding up a little bit of corrugated tin with a slight slope to it. There were no walls but the area under the roof was about five feet by five feet. Out of a few pieces of lumber, someone had built a makeshift bench big enough for two people to sit on.

We planned to do most of our cooking outside, figuring it was smarter and safer than trying to cook in our old, dried-out house. We hoped to make a mud oven within a few days and use it as soon as possible, but in the meantime, we had a primus (kind of like a one-burner camp stove.) Others began clearing a path to our liklik house (an outhouse). I could see that the outhouse was perched on the edge of the back side of the very mountain that we had just climbed up, and I prayed fervently that I wouldn't have to spend too much time in there. I noted with relief that each family's house had its own outhouse nearby, which meant that ours would be for our family's private use.

The liklik house was leaning slightly, but at least it had a black plastic curtain that would give us a degree of privacy. Pieces of plastic were nailed to different parts of the woven walls to cover some of the larger holes. The people proudly showed us how they had sawed an old oil can in half and then cut a hole in the top so that we would have a toilet seat. I began to shoot up prayers right and left: Lord, give me strength, perseverance, and the grace to maintain a sense of humor in all of this. We found out later that the people had burned the oil can (our toilet seat) to sanitize it. For quite a while, the soot from the can left a bull's eye on our backsides.

There were still a lot of people hanging around both outside and inside the house. We thought it best to wait to unpack or cook until we could go through our stuff. Looking back, I can understand why the Lord didn't allow us to bring all of our things when we arrived. Seeing all we had brought would most likely be overwhelming for our visitors. Waiting to eat was hard because our stomachs reminded us that one granola bar each was all we had eaten that day.

Since we didn't feel comfortable eating or unpacking yet, Bill and the boys began to work on a tarp and a bucket to capture rain water, knowing that water would be our number one priority. This crude system ended up being a great blessing to us since it actually worked. With all the rainfall in that area, we usually had plenty of water. In just a few days, we were able to fill our jugs with wonderful, *clear*, cool water.

The people continued to hang around. Around 8 p.m. one young girl must have realized our dilemma. She explained that it was all right for us to go ahead and eat, so we did finally – giving our papa some of the cucumbers Frank had brought up the mountain for us. Papa asked for salt, but we hadn't found it yet. We would soon learn how great a luxury salt was in those parts.

It was dark and as we got ready to cook, we realized that our brand new kerosene lamp didn't seem to be working. We knew it was going to be mighty dark if we didn't have some kind of lantern. Papa gave us his old Coleman to use. We were pretty amazed that he had one and grateful to be able to use it. One thing we've learned as missionaries is that many of the people you're serving think that missionaries have it all together and have everything we could possibly need. Little did we know that our need for a lantern was a good thing. Papa had something we needed and could give it to us. This was important in the Faiwol culture. We saw almost the same thing later in Belize. It made us more dependent on our new family.

Everyone finally tired of watching us and left around 8:30 that night. We started to get organized but were so tired that we finally gave up and prepared to go to bed. We slept under mosquito nets and covered our bodies with a sheet. The sheet served us well as a barrier between our bodies and the bugs that somehow managed to squirm their way through the tiny holes in the net.

Considering the circumstances, it's amazing that we slept as well as we did – that is, until an obnoxious rooster sat himself on the branch of a tree right outside the boys' window and began to crow at 3:30 a.m.! I know that many people in the U.S. still wake up to the rooster's crow, but this was absolutely my first time to have the experience. We've noticed through the years that third world roosters love to wake up Americans bright and early!

20

Feeding the Multitudes

I felt more relaxed the next morning and began to pay attention to the people. They were fairly short, dark-skinned, with kinky hair. We would find out later that there were other language groups of people with much darker skin than the Faiwol – primarily the groups out on the islands. The Faiwol rarely wore shoes and subsequently had very wide, flat feet. They would have had trouble wearing shoes if they'd owned them!

The men generally wore shorts and old t-shirts. The women wore their "meri blouse" – a bell-shaped blouse – that reached past their hips atop a simple a-line skirt. I don't remember ever seeing any women, young or old – wear shorts or pants. Clothes were hard to come by, and most of the people wore the same thing every day.

Several people showed up to visit early that morning but it soon turned quiet in the village as everyone went to their gardens to work, a daily practice, it turned out. We learned to use that time to get our projects done. Part of our jungle camp experience involved making several survey charts, listening to and transcribing local stories and working at learning the language. We looked forward to doing similar homework here because it would teach us more about the Faiwol culture and help us to communicate better.

Later that same first morning, Wade and Chris were hammering on a set of shelves. Some men heard the hammering and came to investigate. Before we knew it, we had six men inside our tiny house all hammering and working. I was under the impression that everyone went to their gardens and wondered where these men had come from. I had planned to cook our big meal at midday to avoid another evening rush, but now we had several hard workers staying on in the house. We were pretty hungry by then.

When I had purchased and planned the food for this trip, it never entered my mind that I would be feeding the whole nation of Papua New Guinea! Over and over in the Bible, we are reminded of God's provision – manna in the wilderness, God providing food to Elijah by means of ravens, the feeding of the five thousand. None of those accounts came into my mind that day. Already thinking of the food that we didn't bring with us and knowing that I had Bill and two teenage sons to feed, I wondered how our rations would hold out. There were a few trade stores in the village. They were about the size of a closet and their stock depended on what had come in on the plane. It was usually hit or miss as far as what you could find – if you could find anything! But I knew that I needed to cook, so I cooked enough rice to serve the 11 people who were now in my house.

We were here to serve the people and to learn from them, but as Americans, we often protected our personal space. Frank had come up the mountain to visit, and being the veteran he is, knew that we needed some time alone. He told the men that we would need to rest for a bit. They smiled and dutifully set off for parts unknown to us after making several shelves in our house. We enjoyed about two hours of quiet and happily greeted the next shift as they came in from their gardens.

As the people arrived, we could see that they had some food with them. I figured that we'd better start learning to live off the land since we were quickly going through our own provisions. The ladies shyly came forward to show me what they had brought – cooked taro, a root vegetable somewhat like a very dry potato and their main source of starch, and some greens that we couldn't identify but that looked suspiciously like a wandering jew plant that would typically turn up in a hanging basket in our home in the States.

Papa showed up and continued to hang around so I knew that I was supposed to serve him some food. Since some of the ladies had so kindly brought us some things from the garden, I was able to share our cucumbers, bananas and taro. Papa left shortly afterwards. Here is where I have to disprove a myth that has developed in the evangelical church – missionaries aren't perfect (and I'm one of the least perfect). I wish I could say that I didn't dwell on our dwindling food supply, but I couldn't help but remember that we had only so much, at this point. I was also very concerned about our getting sick on the local foods so soon into our adventure. A big, big, BIG splish splash!

I could see that feeding portions of the village would likely become a regular occurrence and began to ask God to help me figure out what to do. The pilot had told us that he would bring the rest of our food in "about a week." Since this was my first time at this, I didn't know whether "about a week" was likely to stretch into more.

Our second day came to a close. I was very tired but felt proud that I had survived two full days on the mountain – only four weeks and five days to go. We went to bed about 9 p.m., but didn't get much sleep because a mother pig and her three babies had taken up residence right under our house. The mama pig was using the posts that elevated the house to scratch those hard-to-get spots. We could actually feel the house moving. The pigs kept up their grunting and squealing most of the night. They finally left early in the morning, right about the time the rooster began to deliver his morning wake-up call.

21

The Peeping Toms

On our third night we had a downpour. That was when we discovered the multiple leaks in our tin roof. Around 1:30 a.m. we awoke to find water coming in on top of Wade. We hurriedly moved his bed away from the drippy area to underneath Chris' platform bed to keep Wade dry and prayed that he wouldn't forget where he was and sit up too fast and hit his head. He did fine. Whenever it rained after that, Wade would shove his mattress under Chris' bed. It worked every time.

The rain provided a bonus, however. We were all very excited the next morning to discover that we had captured a whole barrel of rainwater! We eagerly prepared the "closet" so we could start taking showers. In such a hot climate, showers were especially precious and now that we had enough water, we were eager to take advantage of it.

We had brought along a bucket shower which is a two-and-a-half gallon bucket that has a shower nozzle soldered to the bottom. We filled the shower bucket, hoisted the apparatus on a rope pulley and turned on the nozzle. The trick was to get soaped up and rinsed off before all the water emptied from the bucket. The boys laughed and had a great time. They refilled the bucket for Bill while I eagerly anticipated the same refreshment.

It was still light outside when I started my shower. I had just begun bathing when I heard noises below the house. I figured it was the mama pig and her babies again until I heard giggling. Because our house was so old, there were large holes in sections of the outside walls and flooring; and I soon realized that children had gathered under the house and were peering through the holes to see the show! When there's no TV or radio for miles around, I guess you look for your entertainment wherever you can find it. I tried to encourage the growing group of children to go somewhere else. They wouldn't budge. I was committed at that point to finishing up, so I took the fastest shower of my life, grabbed my clothes and got out of there!

The next day, I thought I had figured out a way to outwit my young audience: I would wait until dark. Unfortunately, my fears of the creepy-crawly things began to outweigh my modesty. It was pitch dark in that room, and I had already seen enough six-legged insects to scare me into taking a flashlight with me. I soon found out that a person bathing at night by flashlight is even easier to see through holey walls and floors than someone bathing during the daytime.

I switched to taking showers during the day again, hoping my growing group of thrill-seekers would soon tire of seeing this middle-aged white woman bathe. It became a sort of game with us. I did my best to take showers at a different time each day to keep the young voyeurs from figuring out my schedule. I quickly found out that a good time was earlier in the day when most of the children were with their families in the gardens. Unfortunately, that meant I was bathing early and sweating the rest of the day. Eventually I began to shower in my bathing suit, which eventually brought the adventure to an end.

While the cool showers felt great, I was already beginning to struggle emotionally with life in the village, and I hadn't been there a full week yet!

22

The War with the Bugs

Not only were my showers a challenge but so were the bugs, which were always worst at night. Of particular note were the flying insects that often came out in force after a rain. We were fairly certain that they were some sort of termites living off the remains of the house. Fortunately, they didn't bite us, but they did get into our hair, eyes and clothes as they swarmed all around the house. Sometimes they drove us to an early bedtime. We would give the house over to the bugs, climb under our mosquito nets and talk.

The benefit of having a houseful of bugs, no electricity and little else to do after dark was having valuable face-to-face time with our sons. But even this could turn eventful. One night, after we all went under the mosquito net in our bedroom to enjoy some quality time, we realized we had managed to trap a cockroach in with us, even though we had thoroughly checked the bedding first. As the roach began racing around the interior of the mosquito net, all four of us tore out of there as fast as we could! Later, we collapsed laughing, but I knew there would be thousands more roaches where that one came from!

About a year later, we took videos of what we called the "war between the bugs and us." The video shows the four of us hugging the wall farthest from the lights as the bugs took over the house. At one point, we lit a candle, turned off our solar powered light, and watched the bugs smother the candle within seconds! It was a pretty neat video to show to youth groups when we returned to the States on furlough, but no fun to live through at the time.

Our war with insects was never-ending and usually took us a bit of time to clean up after the evening "bug war." We would actually fill several dustpans with the dead bodies resulting from their kamikaze maneuvers into the candles at night. I have one notation in my journal saying that it took 45 minutes one particular morning to clean up all the bug carcasses. Funny, I couldn't remember anyone mentioning bug clean-up as part of our job description.

The nights were also full of bats. They loved the fig tree right outside our bedroom window. At night we could hear the bats flapping their wings, making a "whoop-whoop" sound as they came in for a landing or take-off. Sometimes one of the village cats would bring a dead bat to our front porch as a trophy. We were never able to figure out how the cats were able to catch them.

Bill knew that the Faiwol people loved to eat bats, so he decided one night to kill one. He felt that he could really show off if he carried a bat to someone – kind of like the cats with their trophies! He went out many a night, sometimes with the boys, but he never once hit or killed a bat.

My reaction to the animals and critters was starting to affect my emotions. As the days went by, I could feel my heart getting hard as I got angrier and more resentful over my situation. It was at this point that I stood on the top of the mountain and wondered how I could feel so miserable in such a beautiful place. I wasn't really seeing the beauty; all I could concentrate on was the dirt, the isolation and the bugs. In hindsight, it reminds me of what happens if you train your eyes on one thing in a room. All the other things seem to blur. That's what was happening to me. The negative things I was focusing on were blocking my view of the marvelous people and the gorgeous, tropical country I was living in. Like Peter, once again, I failed to keep my focus on God (splish splash!).

In spite of our efforts, the bug wars continued. There was a type of wormy, squiggly creature that wiggled through the split bamboo flooring at night. We had no furniture and as we sat on the floor, we could feel these things working their way up the bamboo under us. It was not a comfortable sensation – I hated it! Frank and Charlotte, who were becoming good friends, gave us some old orange cushions. Not only were we grateful to have something soft to sit on, but we now had some protection from what we called "the floor bugs."

Yet there was another buggy area in the house that concerned me even more. A wall that divided the living room from the bedrooms was a favorite place for all the bugs to hide. I was constantly running and screaming as one type of bug or another emerged from this wall. I finally had what I thought was a brilliant idea. I asked Bill to arrange to have the pilot bring us an order of insect repellant when the plane came in with our food. My plan was to soak the wall and kill anything that breathed. It seemed like a foolproof plan to me. Now I was waiting not only for the food that the plane would bring but for the bug spray that I felt would change my life for the better. My focus had shifted from bugs to spray, but it was still not on the Lord.

We thought we had only a week to wait until the next plane arrived, but it was actually two weeks before we saw it again. It's good that we don't know everything ahead of time. When the plane came in, we were excited! In fact, we were starting to understand why all work stopped in the village when a plane arrived. Almost everyone would drop what he was doing and make a mad dash to the airstrip. That

107

day, we were part of the crowd running to the plane, and we weren't disappointed! Not only did we now have some familiar comfort foods, but I had the bug spray. I could hardly wait to saturate the wall.

We climbed back up the mountain and went straight into the house. All of us were watching as Bill began to spray. To my horror, hundreds – and I am not exaggerating – perhaps thousands of creatures began to pour out of this wall: centipedes, a scorpion, cockroaches, and spiders. Bill was killing everything in sight with whatever he had in his hand. Our two boys were roaring with laughter. They, too, without television, were enjoying any entertainment that came their way. Meanwhile, I was screaming my head off!

Several people from the village ran to the house to check on us and later told us that when they heard me screaming and Bill pounding, they were sure that he was beating me for not cooking properly or some other failure. I'm not sure which would have been worse – the beating or the bugs.

23

The Outhouse

By now, my resentment was building rapidly. I resented everything and everyone, including God. "I just knew it," I told Him. "I knew that I could never survive. I knew that I wasn't cut out for this. Why did You ever bring me here? To ridicule me? To have people spy on me while I bathe? To terrify me?" God seemed silent to me during that time. I became distant with my own family and the people around me as I tried to endure those days.

And we hadn't even begun our ministry yet! Village living was a time of testing – testing to see if we would be able to adapt to a village environment. Our only responsibilities these five weeks were to survive and complete some homework assignments. And yet, I was already questioning the calling that God had given me to be there. After all, how could He use someone with a history like mine? I took time to think back over my childhood and early adulthood, not finding anything there that could remotely suggest that I would ever succeed at this. What was God thinking? Didn't He remember my difficult past? But here I was – attempting to serve Him in one of the most remote parts of the earth. I was concerned that my lack of good spiritual upbringing would affect my role as a missionary. Once again I was in the pattern of putting my faith in myself and my own accomplishments, instead of in the Lord.

To top it all off, there was still the liklik house (the outhouse) to contend with. As I said before, this structure was perched on the top of the mountain, but on a slant, with the door facing sideways. This meant that the visitor had to take a few steps down the side of the mountain and make a sharp right turn to get inside the door.

To complicate the process further, it rained almost daily. The soil was mostly clay, very slippery when wet. I would often head downhill and attempt to stop to make the right turn into the outhouse, only to begin to slide down the mountain. The village children no longer watched me bathe, but gathered around anytime they saw me heading to the outhouse. Believe me, I went there as seldom as possible!

The outhouse smelled awful! The oil drum that served as our toilet seat smiled up at us every time we entered. A swarm of mosquitoes with voracious appetites constantly hovered over the hole, just waiting to bite their victims. The thin plastic sheet that served as a door seldom did its job. Any kind of breeze made the curtain billow, and was always just out of my reach when I was seated on the drum. As if that weren't enough, different critters went in and out on a regular basis.

One day, two weeks into our village living, I entered the outhouse through the plastic curtain and saw what I thought was a very large, bright orange snake slithering out through the back wall! The snake could easily escape because our outhouse was as holey as our hut! I saw this thing several times, but I was the only one who did. Whenever I mentioned it to Bill or the boys, they insisted they had never seen anything like it. The boys began rolling their eyes and looking at me like I was crazy, imagining things!

Fortunately, some time later, this orange creature made an appearance to the rest of the family. It wasn't a snake, after all, but a very large lizard, a fact that brought me little comfort. Apparently I had been focusing only on his tail.

It became more and more difficult for me to go into the outhouse. I especially hated going at night. A flashlight did little to protect me from all the terrors that lurked for me there. Sometimes I preferred to go without the flashlight. Not knowing what was flying or slithering around me was somewhat better than knowing. I began to fear that the outhouse would prove my ultimate downfall. After all the training and preparation, a 16-square-foot thatched building was beginning to conquer me.

My attitude was affecting me, my family, and those around me. My attitude affected me personally in the sense that my feelings were suppressing my desire to get to know the people. I also didn't feel well physically. Because of my attitude, my relationship with Bill and the boys was beginning to suffer. I was either cranky and short tempered with them or unusually quiet and distant. When you are in the midst of coping, you often forget about goals, and I had forgotten. I was in survival mode. I was aware that I wasn't behaving properly but didn't really have the desire to change. To make things worse, it seemed like fewer village people were visiting us. I'm sure that was due mostly to the fact that I was distancing myself from them.

A few months earlier, we had read to our boys *The Hiding Place* by Corrie ten Boom as part of our devotional time. I was deeply impressed by Corrie's sister, Betsie. One portion of the story which really touched me was the account of the sisters' imprisonment in the infamous Nazi concentration camp Ravensbruck. Their one bright spot was a smuggled copy of the Bible to which God had seemingly blinded the eyes of the guards when the Dutch sisters were transported there.

One of the first things Corrie noticed about Ravensbruck was the terrible infestation of fleas in the barracks. Immediately, her sister began to thank the Lord for the fleas, but Corrie felt that Betsie was going too far. She couldn't understand how Betsie could thank God for something so difficult. They both thought about their Scripture reading that morning from First Thessalonians 5:16-18: "Rejoice evermore. Pray without ceasing. In every thing give thanks: for this is the will of God in Christ Jesus concerning you." (KJV)

Reluctantly, doubtingly, grudgingly, Corrie joined Betsie in her prayer of thanks for the fleas. They began to cautiously hold Bible studies at night in the barracks, and soon, so many prisoners were coming that they had to start a second study. Surprisingly, no guards ever came in to stop them or disturb them. Later, they would learn that the guards refused to even set foot in their barracks because of the terrible fleas there!

I was reminded of this story as I dealt with the emotional bombardment of living in Papua New Guinea – anger, fear, despair. Finally, realizing that my focus was impaired, I decided then and there to thank the Lord for the outhouse. I figured if Corrie and Betsie ten Boom could thank God in a Nazi concentration camp, I certainly could thank God in PNG. I tagged on one little prayer, though. I asked God to show me at least one good thing about the outhouse, as He had shown Corrie and her sister about the fleas.

I can't honestly say that I began to feel an immediate change of attitude for the outhouse, but that prayer was a significant turning point in my life, one that has stayed with me until this day. God often uses the very difficult things in our lives to mold us, to change us, and to enrich us. I wondered how God could use this vile little building to enrich my life. I felt it would take a miracle for that to happen. Of course, that's God's specialty.

One week after my prayer, I skidded down the hill and made the sharp turn into the outhouse, pulling back the plastic curtain as I hung onto the side. (By the way, I'm amazed that I never tumbled all the way down that slick mountainside.) As I pulled back the plastic to step inside, a hen came tearing out! She was clucking and running almost as fast as my heart was racing. As my eyes adjusted to the darkness, I glanced in the front corner and there ... was a fresh egg! I hadn't seen a fresh egg since we had come to Papua New Guinea! I was so excited that I scooped up the prize and raced to the house. Several villagers were around, as usual, and were now treated to the sight of a crazy white woman leaping and jumping, hoisting an egg.

As I ran into the house to tell my family what I had found, I realized that the Lord had answered my tag-on prayer: the egg was my miracle and also my physical enrichment. Immediately, I started planning what to do – after all, there were four of us – and gleefully realized that we could have pancakes! The next morning, I made the best tasting pancakes that were ever made on the mountain – we all enjoyed them tremendously. Our family had eaten enough oatmeal for a lifetime. In fact, I don't believe either Wade or Chris will eat oatmeal to this day.

Another amazing thing resulted from this experience. The village children were so delighted to see me happy that they began following the hens around and bringing me at least three or four fresh eggs a week. It was wonderful. I often wonder how different my life in Papua New Guinea might have been had my sweet Savior not led me to refocus.

I received one more outhouse-related blessing from some anonymous benefactors in the village. After watching me slide part of the way down the slope, someone came during the night and secretly carved steps into the side of the mountain and put up a handrail. I like to say that I had the first handicapped-equipped outhouse in Papua New Guinea! It was difficult to realize that I had recently been so bitter in the midst of all the blessings around me. Now, I was filled with gratitude, knowing that the Lord had brought me to this outhouse and all the lessons that came along with it. Nothing had really changed as far as my surroundings were concerned. What had changed was my heart and what my heart was focusing on.

24

Getting to Know the People

The recent change in my heart helped me begin to love the Papuan people and the area where we lived. How could I have missed the fact that it was one of the most beautiful settings in the world, with lush, tropical, green mountains surrounding us? I even noticed that if I stood outside the outhouse and looked out across the gorge, there was a waterfall that cascaded about 200 feet down the mountain – one of the most marvelous sights I've ever seen. Wouldn't it would be wonderful to hike to that waterfall sometime? How had I missed seeing it before?

Now that I was looking through God's eyes, I started to see so much more. I began to realize how amazing the village children were. It was fascinating to us to see the children make and play with their own toys. They would take an empty plastic rice bag, for example, fill it with dirt, and transform it into a soccer ball. Of course, when it hit you, their soccer ball hurt much worse than the store variety, but we saw few store-bought balls in the village.

Marbles were small, round stones found lying around the village. Another great homemade toy was a wheel fashioned from a tin can. The children loved to push the can with a stick and often spent quite a few fun hours playing this way. You would think perhaps they had seen the same old black-and-white TV shows that I had seen as a girl and that featured similar kinds of toys. But, without electricity, watching TV was out of the question. Nevertheless, I came to realize that children have similar toys throughout the world.

We had some coloring books, crayons and bubbles with us. We spent hours with the kids – and adults – having great fun sharing these simple pleasures. It was also a good experience for our boys to learn how much fun they could have inventing and designing their own toys.

One particular skill that amazed us was the village kids' ability to make replicas of the different airplanes that landed at the government air strip. They used wood of the sago palm (similar to balsa wood) for the body and wings of the plane, fashioning it into shape with discarded razor blades. Thorns from the sago palm kept the plane together.

We enjoyed hiking around to visit the people with several children usually accompanying us. They loved to point out the various animals and fruits around us. There were times, I have to admit, that I resented the fact that we were rarely left alone. It wasn't until sometime later that I realized many of these children were sent by the villagers to make sure the "white skins" didn't do anything foolish.

One hike was particularly memorable. One member of our "secret service" group was a boy around four or five years old. I loved spending time with him, plus he helped me a lot with my language skills. On one of our hikes he pointed out a really nice red berry. I ate one and loved it! When you are hiking around in 90-plus-degree weather with 90-plus -percent humidity, anything wet and juicy becomes especially delightful. I began eating quite a few berries, so cool and wonderful on such a hot day.

As we continued our walk, I ate more and more. After a while, this little boy tugged on my skirt and indicated to me, with a very serious face, that if I ate any more of those berries I wouldn't be able to use the bathroom for a very long time! While the thought of avoiding the outhouse was tempting, I decided to proceed cautiously. I was grateful for the warning and heeded his advice. Our "secret service" had protected us well.

When we got back from our hike I decided to do some baking. I was developing unique cooking skills. At Jungle Camp, we had learned how to heat up rocks to cook with a contraption called a bake-n-fry. I dug a hole outside in the little hauskuk (kitchen) and gathered up rocks and whatever paper I could find to help start the fire. I was able to get the fire going nicely, hot enough to heat up the rocks.

That day, I planned to make some banana bread. I had been using a recipe without eggs, but now, because of my blessed experience in the outhouse, I was able to add fresh eggs. After getting the rocks and then the pan nice and hot, I poured the ingredients into the pan and found I had time to catch up on some Faiwol stories while waiting for the bread to bake. I was beginning to enjoy talking to the people who frequently gathered to watch me cook, even though we had to use the Pidgin language. Many of their stories revolved around the spirit world, and my sessions became a good way to learn about their fears and beliefs. Afterwards we were able to share some great banana bread.

Once my focus shifted more to others than myself, I was able to take a good look at the children around us. Many had grossly distended bellies. I had seen pictures of such children in magazine ads asking for financial aid, but my reaction to seeing them in real life was much stronger.

I learned later that their belly distention was most likely from worms. Apparently almost all the children had them. On top of that, almost every child had mucus coming from both nostrils, a condition that the Australians in the area referred to as "number elevens." It was very obvious that the villagers were not overly healthy. The average life span in our area was estimated to be about 40 years. I suppose that made me ancient, since I had celebrated my 40th birthday just months before arriving!

Many of the kids and adults also suffered from head lice, a problem so pervasive that most of the villagers shaved all their hair off. Wherever we walked, we would see people on the side of the trails looking through each other's hair for lice. Though I wore my hair long, I never did get lice there. Nevertheless, the children would check me from time to time as they checked each other. I always thought it was sweet that they included me as part of their family.

As I mentioned earlier, the people were fairly short. Whenever I look over our group photos from Papua New Guinea, I get amused. In my own family, I'm the oldest and shortest of six children, but in pictures taken of me with our Faiwol family, it appears as if I'm towering above everyone. It is the only time in my life I have felt tall at 5'4".

Most of the people didn't know exactly how old they were unless they had a government shot record or some sort of birth record. When they did tell me their approximate age, I was always surprised because they appeared older than their age, perhaps as a result of their difficult lifestyle.

One thing that stands out clearly in my mind is their smiles. I loved to see their white teeth flash in their beautiful brown faces. Their sense of humor was very different from ours, however. They would roar with laughter as they recounted stories that involved something gory. The gorier the story, the more they laughed. They would roll on the ground and, if someone added more blood to the story, the laughter would build.

It was good to look at the people with fresh eyes and begin to celebrate occasions and events with them. We celebrated our first Easter in April 1990 by setting the alarm to be up in time for the sunrise service. We didn't end up needing the alarm – the rooster got us up at 5 a.m. As we got dressed, I realized that many people in the States were going to show up at church in their new Easter clothes. We didn't have anything new – just our regular clothes – but that was not important to us in our new setting.

That Easter morning, the trail must have been extra slick because I made a special reference to it in my journal. I also noted the Easter service ran for about six hours. We sang quite a few songs, had different times of prayer, listened to several people preach, and enjoyed a meal together. Afterwards, we spent a few extra enjoyable hours with some of the villagers before heading back up the mountain at 4:30 that afternoon.

It wasn't quite so hot by the time we came up, and I noticed that I fared so much better climbing without the sun beating down on my back. I made a mental note not to scale that mountain at midday anymore but to come up early in the morning or late in the afternoon. It made a big difference!

A few nights later we lay awake and listened to a man singing for several hours. We got hardly any sleep. We were never able to figure out what he was singing nor why, but wondered if he was attempting to ward off evil spirits. While I lay in bed contemplating that, a huge grasshopper landed on my head and scared me to death. Of course the rooster was up at 5 a.m. and so were we. This was my new life – filled with change and adventure. I was taking baby steps in understanding and appreciating the people God had placed before me.

A week after my outhouse experience, we realized that we had been surrounded by people almost constantly for the three weeks we had been in the village and decided that it would be great to sneak off as a family to a little cascade area we had seen not too far away. We knew that we were likely to wind up with someone along with us, but thought it was worth a try. Most of the time we didn't mind the company, but we really did feel the need for some family time.

It took some planning on our part, but we managed to get off by ourselves. We reached the cascade area and found the water deliciously cool and refreshing. Some boys showed up to fish, and our boys enjoyed playing ball with them. Though we weren't alone anymore, it was nice to see Wade and Chris enjoy the company of some of the kids from the village. The Papua New Guinea boys had very little down-time once they hit their pre-teens because they were so busy helping their fathers. Apparently these two had managed to steal away from their chores.

From the shallow water, they began scooping up rocks of varying shades of browns, reds and oranges. They taught us how we could rub them to produce several different colors. We all loved the "coloring" rocks. They were pretty and unique, so we picked up some to take back with us. The boys explained that the people used the rocks to decorate their bows and arrows, shields, and door posts. Their carvings and paintings were beautiful and each of the colored pictures had significance.

Later on, someone made a shield for us bearing many of those significant markings. Bill sat down with the man who made the shield, asked him to explain what each marking meant, and wrote it all down. Some of the markings represented a python, a fern tree, a fish and even a belly button!

The boys continued explaining more uses for the coloring rocks, including painting their faces for singsings. We hadn't experienced a singsing yet. These usually took place during certain holidays or festivals when adults and teenagers dressed up in their traditional clothes and danced. It was so fascinating to look at the stones and realize that we were staring at something that had been used for centuries in Faiwol celebrations. We couldn't wait to see them put to use.

We enjoyed the village boys. They seemed to enjoy us, too, and spent some time showing our two boys how to fish with spears. We made it back from the cascades that afternoon without injury; by contrast, there seemed to be all sorts of hazards in the village. Almost everyone went barefooted, and people often hurt themselves by stepping on the cans, nails and other debris left lying around. It was inevitable that people got hurt.

One afternoon a young girl stepped on a nail. Someone brought her to me, and I cleaned up the wound as best as I could and bandaged it. This was the first time anyone had come to us for help. I was glad to help the girl and told her that she should come back the next day so that I could clean the wound again. She had no shoes and would need to have the dressing changed regularly. I knew that she most likely had never had a tetanus shot and prayed that she wouldn't suffer any problems.

25

Papa Smurf

Papa came to visit right around dinnertime that evening. It was always interesting to have him around as he shared stories while we shared food. It wasn't too great a coincidence that Papa always seemed to appear around a meal time, and I continued to marvel at how far our food extended, because we were always feeding others. I was beginning to relate to the feeding of the five thousand.

Because our Papa was so short, our boys took to calling him Papa Smurf between themselves. He had a unique look. On the bottom of his nose – his septum – he had a large hole which had accommodated boar tusks in his prime.

Wanting to draw something, Papa borrowed a pen from one of our boys, made his drawing, and then absently began to run the pen back and forth through that hole in his nose. With my eyes, I expressed to my sons that they should not start laughing. To their credit they controlled themselves in Papa's presence, but I have to admit that it was very difficult to concentrate with that pen going in and out. Eventually, Papa offered the pen back to us, but we all quickly answered him saying that the pen was his to keep.

While Papa was still sitting with us, I looked out our little window and saw three teenage boys shivering under the eaves of our house. It was raining and the temperature had dropped a little. I doubt that it was any cooler than 80 at the time, but the Faiwol people were accustomed to the extreme heat, and the wet, cooler weather always seemed to bother them. We had the boys come inside and gave them some towels and books to look at. I couldn't stand to see them cold.

While the children were still inside reading, a family sent us some bananas by one of their young sons. We found out that this boy was from the family of the girl who had recently stepped on the nail. I had given their daughter some medical help and now they were showing their thanks with the bananas.

Culturally, the Papua New Guineans keep account of their giving this way. If they give you something it usually means that they are hoping to start a relationship with you. It is a reciprocal arrangement. If someone gives to you, you need to make note of it so that you can give back to him later on. We had learned about this in our Jungle Camp training and were told that we shouldn't try to pay for food or services if it came in this manner because it could damage relationships. We should, however, keep account of who gave what to us and then sometime later make sure to take something to them. Papa had other ideas.

We believe that Papa initially "adopted" us because he felt he and the rest of the villagers would gain something from it. He not only expected to get something for himself but had expressly told us how much we should pay for everything that we received. Papa demanded that we find the boy and pay him for the bananas. That concerned us because we knew that it went against the grain culturally and we hoped to start building healthy relationships with the people in the village. We were concerned that we would be viewed only as rich Americans if we started paying for everything.

Because Papa was so adamant, I went to the young boy's house to offer payment to the family. His mother came to the door and firmly refused any kind of payment. We knew that this girl's family was thanking us by giving to us. I planned to go to their house in a few days with a small gift for them. It would be the start of a new relationship.

When I returned, Papa asked how much I had paid for the bananas. When he found out that I still hadn't paid anything, he was very angry and sent someone from his family to ask about it. They came back and confirmed what we had told Papa – the giver didn't want any money. We were grateful that Papa seemed satisfied with their answer.

There was so much more to learn, and we had to lean on the Lord more and more for wisdom in a new and confusing culture. We were aware that we were often laying the groundwork for important future relationships and prayed that we would always do the right thing. The young girl came again the next day for me to change the dressing on her foot. Thankfully I could see that her foot was healing well. I enjoyed getting to know her as she came back for the next few mornings. We were eventually able to develop a good rapport with her family.

The days seemed to fly by during our village living experience. So many good things were happening. I continued to reap the benefits of having fresh eggs several times a week. The hen continued to cooperate and I allowed her a space in the outhouse. Every time I stepped into the outhouse I would look for my fresh egg, and began to save some for special occasions. How wonderful it was for the Lord to bless me through something that had originally seemed like such a burden.

Even though I regularly got eggs from the outhouse, the kids continued to supply me with more. I guess they thought there was something magical in them since my personality had changed dramatically. I often encouraged the kids to eat the eggs, explaining to them that they were a good source of protein, but they really didn't like to eat them. I think they took a greater enjoyment in making me happy after seeing me so unhappy before.

Though fresh eggs were rare, fresh meats and vegetables were rarer. Because of that, it was always exciting to have one of the planes come in. The SIL planes were a blessing to us. Not only did they fly us in and out of the village but they also usually arrived with some fresh items that we had ordered, plus our mail.

We had been told early on that our village wasn't a favorite of the pilots, for several reasons. One reason was that the fish bowl we lived in allowed only one way in or out through the break in the mountains. Not only were we in the fishbowl, but the clouds tended to come in most afternoons and fill the area where the air strip was located, making visibility almost non-existent.

Because our village was a two-and-a-half hour flight from Ukarumpa, the Wycliffe base, the pilots often found themselves trying to come in at the time the clouds started forming. Many times, Bill helped guide down the planes using the radio inside our house. On these occasions, Bill's years in the Air Force came in very handy. Because he is also very directionally oriented, Bill could hear the plane, crane his neck to look out the window for any openings in the clouds, and direct the pilot towards the nearest opening. Several pilots made it into the village and found themselves unable to get back out. They would spend the night with us and fly out again the next morning. One of the pilots laughingly told us that they drew straws when it was time to come to our village. The loser had to make the trip!

We were the last stop on the flights that came our way. That meant that when we needed a flight, others could piggyback on it to get their mail and provisions, but we weren't always that lucky. The pilots weren't always able to get out to our village. Because we were the final stop, mail seemed to take forever to get to us. It took a good two to four weeks for the mail to get to Papua New Guinea from the United States, and then it might take an additional four to six weeks to get to us in the village.

26

The Plane! The Plane!

As I mentioned, when we first got to Kungabip we noticed that when the planes came in everything else stopped as the villagers ran down to the airstrip. We found this puzzling at first because we might be in the middle of a conversation or language learning and whoever we were with would set off running. It didn't take long, however, until we were part of the regular group charging down the mountain to see what plane was landing and why.

Not only the Wycliffe/JAARS planes came in, but MAF (Missionary Aviation Fellowship) and local airplanes flew in as well. We saw surprised looks on pilot's faces more than once as they stepped out of their planes, looked around at the crowd of short, dark-skinned people and suddenly spotted our comparatively tall, white bodies!

We were really looking forward to the next plane. It was due to come in with more of our food,

Chris' guitar, the precious mail and some other items. On the way down the slippery mountain to the airstrip, a lady with several of her kids caught up to us. She slowed her pace to match ours. I'm sure that she could have gone much faster, but stayed with us, even though we didn't talk much because of the language barrier. She was taking on the responsibility of watching out for us. It's probably a good thing that the villagers did watch out for us because so much could have gone wrong. Plus, they also gave us plenty of opportunities to work on learning the Faiwol language.

Having the plane come in was like Christmas. We never really got over that feeling. As time went on, whenever the plane came in, we would take the rest of the afternoon off just to put things away, read all the mail and enjoy seeing what had come. We never felt guilty about that because we didn't have regular hours anyway. We worked hard when we worked and enjoyed the down time when the plane came in. We were starting to adopt the perspective of many around us.

Among the things that arrived on this particular plane were my hiking boots. I could hardly wait to use them, thinking that they would help me up and down the mountain. I had been wearing sneakers up to this point and felt that their tread contributed to the slipperiness of the somewhat steep incline.

The local people were much more agile, even though barefooted. Their feet were wide and thick and had adapted over the years to their environment. I was afraid to go barefoot, although Bill and the boys did many times. I kept thinking about all those pigs that just ran loose and the pig stuff I might be stepping on, not to mention rusty cans or trash. So I usually kept shoes on.

I excitedly tried on the boots as I prepared for my next trip down the mountain. Here was the answer to all of my problems on the trails! Yes, the cleats on the boots did seem to hold better, but there was now a bigger problem. The clay was so thick that it rapidly built up on the cleats, and soon I was carrying around about an extra five to ten pounds of clay on each boot. My feet felt heavier and heavier. Eventually I ended up with such a thick layer of clay that the boots became more slippery than the tennis shoes! I soon reverted to tennis shoes unless the ground was very dry – which wasn't often. Sometimes I was brave enough to go barefoot, but I never mastered it like the men in my family did.

Now that both boys had their guitars, they often played them outside while we were spending time with the people in the village. What a great ice breaker! The people loved to listen to the music. I'm sure they had never heard the songs or the tunes being played before, but they listened intently.

133

27

Relationships

It was nice being adopted into the tribe. When we first arrived we didn't quite know what to make of it, but soon found out that our "parents" took their role as our caretakers very seriously. In reality, both our "mama" and "papa" were probably close to our own ages. They were very involved in the village church and Mama, in particular, seemed to be very much in love with Jesus. That might explain why they were so willing to take us in. Papa was the village leader, called a Council, equivalent to a mayor. So, when he said we were family, we were family! We were also the first "white-skins" to live in their village, although Frank and Charlotte had lived in a neighboring village for many years. Mama, in particular, would check on us regularly to see if we were okay and would often bring us some local fruits. Eight children of their own and they still took us on!

I remember one day Mama brought us a large chunk of lean pig. We were very touched by the gift. We knew how little protein the Faiwol people got and always felt guilty taking any meat from them. We often would reciprocate with things that we had in our own inventory, trying to make sure that we were giving something nutritious in return. The day that Mama brought us the delicious pork was a day that we had planned to eat only some two-minute noodles, so it was greatly appreciated.

We didn't usually eat the food that Mama brought right away because we preferred to soak it if it was produce or cook it some more if it was meat. Even though the pork Mama brought us that day was already cooked, I cooked it again to make sure that we didn't get sick eating it. It tasted wonderful, not only because we knew how generous Mama was being but also because most of our recent fare had been either canned or dried.

The same day that Mama brought us the pork another lady brought us cucumbers. My reciprocity list of giving was getting longer. I could no longer keep tabs mentally but made notes as to who had given us what. I'm not sure how the Faiwol kept up with what seemed to me to be a complicated system, but I wanted to be certain I never left anyone out.

Returning favors was challenging sometimes because we had to identify the people who had "favored" us. We weren't usually told people's names, but rather their relationship to us. Therefore we would be introduced to our aunt, our cousin, our brother-in-law. They didn't even tag on the name after the title like we do when we say, "Aunt Mary" or Aunt Kathy," but would simply call a woman "aunt." So, relying on titles was no help. Sometimes I would note which house a gift-giver had come from, but often I had no clue where he lived.

One great way to keep up with the people was by the clothes they wore. As I mentioned before, they had few clothes, so we could identify the people by their t-shirts. Thus, we might privately call someone "blue and white shirt" or "green pants with yellow stripes." It sounds like a crazy, complicated way to keep up with people but it worked, probably because the villagers wore the same clothes day after day. Thank goodness they didn't swap clothes often!

To maximize our free time to visit with the people, I cooked the majority of our large meals outdoors at midday. We still had only the little primus to cook on in the house. We had originally planned to use it often, but it wasn't working. We needed a screwdriver to fix it – another item we didn't have. This made breakfast challenging, to say the least. We usually managed to find some way to heat water, and I guess that is why we ate so much oatmeal. We also continued to cook on the heated rocks with our "bake and fry" method. Eventually we made our mud oven and cooked in that, as well.

We went down the mountain and borrowed a screwdriver from Frank Mecklenburg sometime later. I still don't know how we would have managed those first few weeks without him. We knew when we arrived in Olsobip that Frank would be in the village only for the first couple of weeks, since Charlotte was soon returning from the States. Since she would fly into Ukarumpa, the Wycliffe center, Frank planned to travel there to be with her and would stay for several weeks. Right now, he was a lifesaver!

While we were at Frank's borrowing the screwdriver, he suggested that we move into his house for the rest of our village living phase while he and Charlotte were in Ukarumpa. He felt that it would be easier for us and that we would also be closer to the majority of the people we were working with. We were torn as we made our decision. The issue was not that we would be so far from our Kungabip village family, but that we would be down the mountain from them and not actually in their village.

We knew everyone came down from their mountains and passed through the area where Frank's house was located on their way to the gardens. We didn't think the move would hamper our ability to spend time with the people. We also thought about the living conditions where we were and decided that we might fare a little better at Frank's. Nevertheless, it was a very hard decision to make. We contacted our leaders from Jungle Camp by radio to ask them what they thought. They agreed that staying at the Mecklenburgs' would be a good idea. However, we didn't make the move right away.

We also had to consider where we would live when we returned to the village to begin our "official" ministry. There was an empty house that had been used for the literacy worker, Mila. It was small by U.S. standards, twenty feet by twenty feet, about the size of a two-car garage. Though it was twice as big as our Kungabip house, we weren't sure how we could all manage living in it. The house was made out of sawn lumber from the local sawmill that the villagers operated for literacy funding. The roof was corrugated tin. Each side of the house had two windows. All of the windows were boarded up and there was neither glass nor screens on them. I made a mental note, after our history with bugs, that louvered glass and screens would need to be ordered before we could live there.

The inside was barren. There were no finished walls, only studs. There were only three rooms: one we would later use for a kitchen, one which would become a bedroom, and the other which would be made into two rooms – a living room/dining room combination and a bathroom. Speaking of bathrooms, an outhouse, nestled among overgrown weeds, sat right outside our new home, beckoning me to enter. I hoped it wouldn't be often!

The house had been vacant for a while and needed lots of repair. We didn't have enough money to build anything from scratch so it seemed the only choice we had. Frank and Charlotte invited us to stay in their house while they were away from the village, and while we made repairs on the literacy house.

In the meantime we were still living in Kungabip and wanted to take advantage of our time. Many afternoons, after the people started coming back from their gardens, I would sit outside so I could talk with people. Usually, the teenage girls came and sat with me. The married ladies were generally too busy to just sit and chat. To talk to them I had to go to their houses while they busied themselves cooking what they had brought back from the gardens.

I learned a lot from the teenage girls. They were always eager to talk about their customs and learn about ours. They were curious about our family, specifically Bill. They had seen him always carrying the heaviest load and helping me around the house. One day, one of the girls asked me what magic I had used on him to get him to help out so much. I laughed and said that he came like that! They were very impressed.

One interesting custom I learned about from the girls involved the bride price. It was practiced among most of the Papua New Guineans, including the Faiwol people. When a young man wanted to marry a certain young woman, his family would call a meeting with her family. This meeting could take quite a while and involved a lot of ceremony. The girl's family told the boy's family what they required as a bride price. For all intents and purposes, the boy and his family were buying the girl.

Specific items were used to pay for the bride. The price usually involved several pigs, more for monetary purposes than food; string bags that the people called bilums; cowry shells which were often made into necklaces; pig tusks, and more recently, axes. We learned that actual money exchanged hands sometimes, but this was very rare. I guess monetary exchanges were saved for the richer families.

After much negotiation, the "price" would be settled on and worked out. Once the price was paid or almost paid off, the "bride" would move in with her new "husband." In our area, at least, there was never any ceremony. The pair just moved in, but their commitment to the marriage was strong. We never heard of divorce, although there were some couples who no longer lived together.

There were some instances of polygamy. I met two women in Loubip who were married to the same man, and who told me how the arrangement worked. The younger woman did most of the chores and kept her husband satisfied. We talked for quite a while and laughed quite a bit as I told them that I wouldn't want to share my husband with anyone. They thought that was pretty funny.

28

I Thought it Would be Me Falling Apart!

Our little one-burner primas broke again. Because it was all that we had to cook on without starting a fire, it was indispensable. I never mastered cooking on a fire. Our little kitchen area was in the open and we were unable to cook there when it was raining because of the leaky tin roof that covered it. The same day that our primas broke, one of our boys accidentally broke the glass on Papa's lantern, which didn't work well anyway. Within the next 24 hours, somehow the glass broke on one of our own small lanterns. Our pricker, the little tool that we used to light up the primas, also broke.

To make matters worse, we also broke our fly swatter! We had killed too many bugs with it. While Bill was working on the broken fly swatter, he cut his finger TWICE! He already had a small hole in his finger where a saksak needle had entered it. Saksak was what the villagers called the sago palm tree, and it had needles on it. I can't remember why Bill was messing with the tree, but somehow he got one of the needles in his thumb. And if that were not enough, he also burned his big toe on the bake-n-fry which I was using to cook on in the corner of our house (it was raining outside) while he was trying to fix the broken primas.

Days like this would become the norm in our missionary lives during our term in Papua New Guinea and later during our nine years in Belize. Sometimes we rode through the events well, able to laugh about them. At other times, we struggled through every little problem. This was one of the laughing times. Most of my humor was based on the fact that I had thought I would be the one who would fall apart on the field. It seemed that Bill was taking on my role quite nicely. He had some sort of boo-boo on several parts of his body. I, however, was fairly well intact.

In spite of these minor calamities, we continued to work on the homework we had been assigned to accomplish during our village living phase. One assignment was to record and transcribe a story. Another major assignment was to fill out a kinship chart showing how the villagers were related to each other. Both assignments sound fairly easy, as I write this, but in reality, they weren't easy at all!

My favorite time of the day continued to be the late afternoons. We would busy ourselves in the morning and early afternoons doing our assignments, reading, or hiking. But I still loved sitting outside as the people came back from their gardens. It was a cooler time of the day, a wonderful time to get to know people better. Because they did not have any responsibilities, it was easy to interact with the kids any time of day, but the parents were so busy trying to take care of their families that they had little free time.

I figured that I should get started on the projects and develop relationships at the same time. At this point I don't think that people stopped to visit because of any real friendships but out of curiosity. As we began to talk, I realized that completing the kinship chart would be a significant challenge. Just about everyone was related to someone else in the village in several ways. The intertwined relationships didn't fit our chart and seemed complicated to us foreigners. The villagers, however, didn't have any problems figuring it out at all. In fact, they were able to tell me exactly how they were related to each other.

I decided that it was important to figure out how I was related to the people I was meeting so that I could address them properly. After all, we had a mama and a papa. But with some of my "interviewees," I would just have to ask them, "What do I call you?" They were always gracious enough to tell me. Sometimes I would hear something like, "Oh, I'm your mother's sister's child's son. You would call me *nephew*."

Obtaining a story and putting it down on paper was another challenge. I had to have someone tell me a story in Pidgin, since we weren't proficient enough to do anything in Faiwol. We had to tape record the person's story and then translate it into English.

I met a man who told me an interesting story about a woman in the garden. It was filled with the usual gory stuff. I worked hard on the taped version, dutifully copying it down in English. I didn't understand portions of the story, including the ending. I started and stopped that tape countless times as I worked feverishly to get it all down.

Once I had finished, feeling rather proud of myself, I read the story back to the story teller in English. He knew English fairly well because he worked at the government site. It turns out that I had missed various crucial twists and turns of the story and missed the moral of the story entirely. That was somewhat frustrating but also enlightening as I realized how easy it would be to misunderstand or misinterpret other more important things being said. Bill had heard the same story a totally different way, as well. The lessons I learned from this experience stayed with me in the different cultures I lived in. It helped me to realize why it is easy to offend someone in another culture when key words are misinterpreted.

29

Knock, Knock

As I got braver and ventured out to people's homes more, I learned that the ladies sat in their kitchens a good part of the time when they weren't in their gardens. Peeking inside a hauskuk, you would see mostly women, some children, a few pigs and maybe a cat. A fire was going almost all the time. For the first six months or so, as I approached the hauskuks to visit some of the women, I would call out to them from outside. I had already learned from visitors coming to our house that no one ever knocked on a door. There was a kind of "door etiquette" we learned fairly early on. Usually someone would come up and whistle a tune or clear their throat. They rarely called out to us. It wasn't like life in the States where our houses are so enclosed that we don't even hear a car drive up. Our house was open and very small. It wasn't too hard to hear when people came to the door. It was kind of a nice system.

Whenever I approached someone's house, a "town crier" often ran ahead of me to let the person know I was on my way, so I rarely needed to cough or whistle. Someone was often standing at the door to greet me. After several visits I realized that even though the woman greeting me at the door was friendly, she never invited me in. Instead I would end up standing outside on the steps to talk while the homeowner and other family members stayed inside. Their houses were raised, so that meant that I was standing precariously on the thin little steps they called stairs. Needless to say, I never stayed too long, and my feelings of isolation began to increase.

Not only did I begin to feel more isolated, my feelings were getting hurt! The ladies seemed nice enough, so I couldn't figure out why they would neither come outside to talk to me nor invite me in. I was starting to feel rejected when one day there was a nice group gathered inside a hauskuk. They seemed to be having an interesting conversation and my curiosity got the best of me. My desire to talk to them was so great that I decided to just walk into the kitchen-hut. The ladies didn't seem to mind at all. In fact, they seemed pleased. I left that afternoon feeling much happier and wondering more about their culture.

A few weeks later, when talking to the same group of ladies, I discovered that no one invites a visitor into her house. You are just supposed to walk in if you are friends or family. It turned out that the ladies were thinking that I was the one being standoffish, since I never came into their houses. They thought that perhaps I was afraid of them! I realized how much I still had to learn from these interesting and kind people.

When people visited us, no one came directly into our house because we actually had a door, so they would make their gentle noises outside until we came and opened the door. Now we knew that, because we were friends, they didn't need an invitation to come in. We had no furniture so we sat around on the floor to talk. Later, when we moved into our own little house down the mountain, we had chairs. We would automatically sit in a chair and offer chairs to our visitors, but they almost always refused, choosing instead to sit on the floor – so we got off our chairs and sat on the floor with them.

Even though the people didn't often sit in chairs, there were usually some in each village. It was amazing to us that when we hiked to one of the villages, someone would run to get one or two chairs and bring them to us. If they couldn't find a chair, they would offer us a stump or something to sit on! We always refused the seats because we preferred to sit on the ground with the people. But they never gave up trying to make us feel more comfortable! I learned so much about hospitality from them.

30

Does This Church Service End at Noon?

Thinking of comfortable places to sit reminds me of the church services. They were always interesting. There were only two churches in the village – a Catholic Church and an Australian Baptist Church. Both were situated at the base of the two mountains. While we lived in Kungabip it meant a slick climb down the mountain, but once we moved down into Frank and Charlotte's house and then into our own little house, we lived only a short distance away from the church on the opposite side of the grass airstrip. We would walk down our pathway about one-fourth mile to the airstrip and then across the strip. Then we had just a little way to go to get to the Baptist Church where we worshipped.

This short trek wasn't usually difficult at all – it was all on level ground. What did make it difficult at times was getting more rain than usual. When that happened we had to walk in deep mud the entire way. A particular kind of grass along the route bore seeds that somehow jumped off the grass onto our socks and clothing. They were prickly and quite a nuisance. The Baptist church was only about 20 feet long by 15 feet wide. It could hold 50 to 60 people. There were about 12 "pews" that were really just logs on the ground. I always headed for my special "pew." I liked that particular log best because it was somewhat flat on the top, which made sitting easier. There were no backs on the logs, of course, and because they were at ground level, there was no place for your feet either. Services sometimes lasted a couple of hours or more, so getting the right seat was important to me, although no one else seemed to pay attention to where they sat. I liked to be near a window, because the weather was so hot. At least I could feel some air touching my hot, wet neck when there was a breeze.

The women, their small children, and older daughters sat on the right side of the church, and the men and their sons occupied the other side. Because of this seating arrangement and the fact that the church was often the only place we saw certain people, it took us quite a while to figure out who was married to whom!

Sometimes the services were conducted in Pidgin since we were on a government site. Though we sang most of our songs in Faiwol, the local tribal language, most of the Scripture reading and sermons were in Pidgin. It was exciting to hear the pastor, Finamsep, use portions of the Scripture in Faiwol that the Mecklenburgs and the language helpers had only recently translated.

All the services were fairly long by American standards, but no one seemed to mind. There was a charismatic flair to the services at times, with much emotion. Several people seemed to be genuine Christians, showing the fruit of the Mecklenburgs' labor.

Many times after the Sunday service, we would encounter groups of youth playing sports on the government site. Usually the boys played basketball. The girls and a few women would play volleyball. I love volleyball; it is one of the few sports that I can say I play well. I soon found out that the villagers had their own set of rules. It took me quite a while to figure out what their rules were – I'm not sure that I ever fully understood them. However, I always enjoyed the opportunity to spend time with the young girls and women and get some exercise at the same time.

During one of these times I got to know some of the girls a little better. Georgina, Marie and Marta all told me I could come to their house anytime I wanted to. I invited them to my house as well. I started thinking about how I could start a small Bible study with them, especially since all three understood some English and Pidgin.

I was beginning to realize that the names people gave us were often nicknames, since their birth names were usually very difficult to pronounce or understand. So, even though I had met Georgina, Marie and Marta, it could be that their birth names were very different. I was thankful for some names I could get a handle on, rather than Finamsep, Sakiba, and Amina.

31

Inspection Time

If we wanted to buy fresh produce, we had to go down to the airstrip very early in the morning about once every two weeks. One morning, Bill and Wade went down the mountain to see what they could find. Chris and I stayed home. That day we noticed that quite a few villagers hadn't gone to the gardens and we wondered why not. A little later, two strangers climbed up the mountain and began to gather a crowd around our little outside kitchen, already a nice meeting place since it was where we routinely chatted with the people coming back from gardening. This particular morning it became a meeting place as people gathered around the two men.

Chris and I decided to go outside and find out what was going on. In the absence of world news, little events like this became big news in our lives. I smile now as I write this because I can still remember how we initially thought the people were lazy and thoughtless to drop everything to investigate new happenings. Now we were just as bad, if not worse.

The men, who spoke in Pidgin, were curious about what two tall blond "white-skins" were doing there. After explaining ourselves, we asked the men what they were doing there as well! They told us that they worked for the government and had come to declare that day "Village Clean-up Day." Apparently either this "clean-up day" came on a certain schedule or the people had somehow been notified, because they seemed to know that the officials were coming. The government men told me that they had actually planned a surprise inspection but decided to come on the regular schedule instead and give the village a few days to come up to standards.

The men left some written information, which I thought was very interesting for several reasons. First, most of the people we knew in the village didn't read or write. I guess these officials assumed that someone in the group would be able to read the instructions, and they were right. Also, we were glad to read what was expected because we felt that joining the villagers to clean up would offer us a better opportunity to spend more time with them. The information was interesting enough that I recorded it in my journal:

1. "All houses, hauskuks, and liklik houses have to be cleaned up and repaired.
2. All pigs must be fenced for health reasons.

3. All the youth are leaving the villages to work in the gold and copper mines. We encourage them to stay. (They listed quite a few employable jobs and projects at the government site.)
4. Adultery is not allowed. If a husband leaves his wife, she can collect support for 16 years."

I thought this last item was interesting since very little money exchanged hands in our village. The bartering system was still used extensively. I also wondered how this "alimony" would be paid.

Rule #2 also got my attention. I was quite happy to hear that these officials would check to see that all the pigs would be fenced in, since they were a nuisance to me. I knew that the children and adults went around barefooted most of the time and walked in the pig mess along the trails. I was also tired of hearing the pigs grunting and scratching under our house.

Some cleaning took place that day. It was a good time of working together and learning more about these people I was growing to love, but I have to admit that I was disappointed to find out that the government men never did return to inspect the village. Apparently the villagers knew that they wouldn't come back. They never fenced up the pigs!

A plane came in late that afternoon, around 5 p.m. We were excited because our new lantern arrived on that plane. We had experienced nothing but trouble with all our lamps so far and felt that, finally, we might have some decent light in our hut. Our excitement waned when we discovered that this lantern didn't pump well. The glass cracked almost immediately from the heat. Yet, even without a good working lamp, we still ended up with a fully lit room – not too hard to do when the room measures about six feet by five!

32

Tabubil – The Gold Mine

We were supposed to leave the next day for a trip to Tabubil. We were excited about the chance to go because it sounded like another world, complete with cold sodas and fresh food. A 15-minute flight away, Tabubil was a copper mining town run by Australians and located amid several villages in our language group. It was like a small Australian town in the middle of Faiwol villages. Even though we had to walk almost everywhere we went in Tabubil, it was still an exciting place to go to during that first year in the country.

It poured rain all night the night before and into the next morning. Totally fogged in, we didn't get to make the trip – providential because the boys and I ended up being sick all day. The next day we were feeling better and had started to cook breakfast when a Faiwol woman came running to our door. Apparently, she had run all the way up the mountain from the airstrip. She said that, if we hurried, we could catch an SIL plane to Tabubil! So we put up our cooking utensils, grabbed our bags and started running down the mountain. We were turning into true Faiwol people, ready for adventure at a moment's notice. We had been calling them "minute-men," because when a plane came in, people appeared at the airstrip with packed bags. Now we were a "minute-family!"

The trail that day was in the worst shape that we had ever seen as we scrambled to get down the mountain. It was slippery and steep, but none of us fell. The pilot, Randy, was gracious, quite willing to try getting us to Tabubil. He was even kind enough to fly us around a bit to show us some of the views. He dropped us off in Tabubil and gave us two hours before he would come back. It was a fairly long walk from the airstrip to the center of town where we could find the supermarket and drug store, but we set off happily.

The stores were as nice as or nicer than we had imagined. After living out of boxes and cans, we were overwhelmed by the choices of fresh foods and we stocked up, even buying some fresh hamburger and chicken for our dinner that night, knowing that after we ate these fresh meats we would be back to Spam and dried meat.

The town was incredibly hot. All the roads were made of white limestone/dirt, and the cement made it that much hotter. It also made everything brilliantly white, which was very hard on the eyes. Without ground transportation, we now had to carry our groceries to the airstrip. But we were still very grateful to have the fresh food and figured it was worth the inconveniences. We made it back on time and Randy did too. The flight back was smooth: the sky was starting to cloud up, as it did almost every day, and it rained as we climbed over the mountain to head back home.

That afternoon, after we got back, Mama walked up the mountain with us and gave us an entire bunch of bananas. Jacoby, her oldest son (and our brother) later brought us four pineapples. We had gone from famine to feast. Our Mama knew that we usually didn't have any fresh food and often worried about our running out since we were dependent on planes and had no garden of our own.

In return, we shared some of our fresh meat. It was always exciting to do this because the Papua New Guinean's custom of reciprocal giving fostered the forming of relationships – and lots of that kind of giving seemed to be going on. The more you gave the more chances you had to develop your relationship. Of course, we had to be careful not to give so much that the villagers couldn't reciprocate. There was a real art to this custom and we enjoyed learning it.

We dug into the fresh bananas right away. Eating bananas was a way of life in Papua New Guinea. I have never had a great fondness for bananas, nor has Chris, but I ate them often because I knew that they contained lots of potassium, which is great when you sweat a lot. That day the bananas tasted scrumptious.

Bananas were fairly plentiful. We had two kinds of banana trees in our yard – the regular variety and plantains (cooking bananas). Though we could get bananas whenever we wanted, cutting down a whole bunch wasn't practical since only two members of our family ate a significant number. All the other people in the surrounding villages cut down an entire bunch at a time, but we decided that we should take only part of a bunch, according to how many we needed.

There was an old man who walked down a path through the banana plants, around our house, and off to the gardens almost every morning. He was our neighbor's father, Timothy. Bill and he would exchange a few pleasantries every day – just a few words because Timothy spoke only Faiwol. Timothy would always look around our land as he walked by, and we began to realize that he would stand and look at the banana plants with a puzzled expression on his face. He was trying to figure out why the bananas on the bunch were disappearing little by little! We finally told him we only cut a few at a time rather than the whole bunch. I'm sure that he thought it was odd, but he was kind enough not to say so.

As time went by, we got more and more involved in the literacy work in the village. We had come to Olsobip with the title of Literacy Specialists. Anytime our titles were used, we got amused since we felt like anything but specialists, but we knew that God had us there for a reason. One of our first meetings was a literacy meeting with Mila, the leader of the program, which at one time had 25 teachers, but was now down to six. Mila told us that many had left to work with the oil company in Tabubil or at the gold mine.

I remembered what the government men said about losing the young men to the mines. I knew that the villagers needed money because the economy was changing, and I felt sad because I knew that their culture wasn't necessarily changing for the better, with so many men leaving their families to find work. Later the literacy program would face a crisis, and God saw us through in a miraculous way, but at this early point, we were ignorant of what lay ahead.

33

Tumbling off a Slippery Log

We had been admiring a 200-foot waterfall across the gorge for quite a while. From our perspective it didn't look too far away. In fact, it looked as if we would need only to climb down our mountain, through a very congested valley full of vines and trees, and then back up another mountain to get there. One day, we decided to see if we could get closer to it. We asked Ruth, our aunt, how to get there, and she worked hard to discourage us from hiking to that location. We assured her that if the trip became too hard, we would turn back. I remember a man telling Bill, "You and the boys go, but don't take that woman with you." (He meant me!) As usual, because the gracious Faiwol people never wanted to let us travel on our own, four young children were assigned to be our tour guides.

The trail was terrible – quite steep in places and very muddy. We all had to walk slowly, especially me! We came to one bridge that looked quite intimidating. Actually, I don't know why I'm referring to this as a "bridge." It was really a log, pitched at about a 60-degree angle, which crossed a small ravine. Of course, because of the humid conditions, the log was covered in moss and was quite slick.

I was too afraid to cross this imposing "bridge" on foot, so I started scooting on my bottom. Bill was on foot right behind me and began to wobble. Because I was scooting so slowly, he couldn't run ahead to regain his momentum and balance. He couldn't go anywhere but down! He fell, flipped over and stopped at the bottom – about ten feet below us.

At first none of us could see him, and it took a few seconds for Bill to assure us that he was okay. He had been wearing a bright red Ohio baseball cap that our pastor from the States had given him, and he waved it so that we could see where he was. He told us that he was fine but pretty wet and dirty.

Later, when I had time to reflect on that experience deep in the jungle, it made me think of how we take for granted how wonderfully the Lord protects us daily. If Bill had really hurt himself that day, I have no idea how we would've ever gotten him back up that mountain for help. It was gracious of the Lord to provide so much brush on the way down to soften Bill's fall. He didn't have even a scratch.

Of course, Bill has never let me live it down that I was the cause of this potential disaster, since I had to cross the log in my own special way. After he climbed up out of the small ravine to where we were waiting, and after assuring us all once again that he was really okay, we set off again.

We had already hiked quite a distance and it was definitely looking as if we would never reach the large waterfall that had lured us. However, our young guides kept saying that there was a smaller waterfall not far away. We later learned that there were variations on what the Faiwol people thought was a long way and what we thought was a long way – a big difference!

There was what they called a short way, which we Americans would call a long way. Then there was a kind of long way ("long we liklik" in Pidgin English) which we Americans would call a great distance. And when the Faiwol said something was "a long way true," we would call it ridiculous and wait for transportation.

The children had told us that the smaller waterfall was a "long we liklik." That meant maybe two to three hours for them, and approximately ten hours for us tender-feet, we later came to realize.

We walked on for several hours. We never knew how close we might have come to that waterfall but realized, when all we could still see was more jungle in front of us, that we needed to turn back if we were going to return to Kungabip before nightfall.

Even though we never reached the waterfall, it was nice walking and talking with the kids. One young girl, Sara, really caught my heart. She appeared to be about nine or ten years old. She had never started school, but hoped to the next year. She told me how much she wanted to learn how to read. Many of the girls, though, never got to go to school because they were so necessary at home.

Another of our young guides disappeared during our trek, shortly after Bill's fall. We didn't really think anything of it, figuring that she had probably just gotten tired. It turns out that she was the town crier and had run ahead of us, telling everyone about Bill having fallen. When we got back, many people came to see if he was all right.

What is really interesting is that some of the people actually thought that I was the one who had fallen. I wasn't glad that Bill had fallen, but I *was* glad that I had proven myself that day to those who had advised Bill not to take me on the trip. The villagers never again told Bill not to take me along with him, and I accompanied him on almost every hike that he took during our term. It was a wonderful feeling to have established that I was capable of strenuous exertion. The fall didn't seem to cast a dark cloud on Bill's abilities, but I still think that if I had been the one to fall that day, I might never have gained the villagers' approval for future trips.

I sat down with Sara for a while when we got back to teach her a little reading, beginning with vowels. She was excited and planned to come back the next day. I had very little training in this area and wished that I had some idea of how to teach a child to read. I couldn't remember how I learned to read. And I was called the Literacy Specialist! But the Lord is gracious and helped me along as I struggled to do things I felt I had absolutely no skills for.

Most of our evenings were filled with people coming to visit. I have a note in my journal concerning the day Frank Mecklenburg came to visit. Shortly after he left, Papa came, then another "big" man, a village tribal leader. This first group of visitors stayed for quite a while and then my "pikinini" (the word used for children) friends came. A little later, Ruth, Papa's sister, came as well. It was 8 o'clock that evening before I even started preparing our light meal.

34

Did Anyone See a Flying Alarm Clock?

Not only was Papa notorious for showing up at our hut at dinnertime, but he also usually stopped by around 6 o'clock or so every morning before he took off for the gardens. We were fairly used to his visits now. The rooster always made sure that we were up! One morning Papa announced that, in honor of our move down the mountain, his family would kill the rooster that had been keeping us up every night. His oldest son, Jacoby, set out with his bow and arrows while Mama went along with a big stick. A pretty good sized crowd gathered to see what would happen. It looked like a lot of noisy fun.

Mama was actually the one who stunned the rooster; then others in the group began to beat on him with sticks. Up to this point, the only dead chicken I had ever seen was nice and clean and frozen in the freezer section of my local grocery store. Watching the rooster being hunted down and killed was difficult for me, and I tried to keep from seeing too much of it.

The rest of the people, however, seemed to enjoy all the noise and the thrill of the chase!

Once the rooster was dead, Mama picked him up by his two feet and handed the unlucky bird to Chris. At the same time, several people simultaneously began to tell me how to prepare him. They told me that I would need to build a fire and hold him close to the fire in order to singe his feathers off. Then I would need to pluck him and clean him out. All of that was to be done before any cooking started.

I was horrified to think that I was going to have to cook this rooster! All sorts of thoughts ran through my head, including the strong desire to run in the other direction. The look on my face must have given me away, because Mama said that she would handle the preparations. I felt relief and even had a minute to think about how wonderfully quiet the next morning would be without the crowing rooster.

A few hours later, Mama proudly brought us the cooked rooster. She had cooked the stomach along with the poor guy, which left him really gritty. It was dark by the time she brought him, and in the weak light of our lantern we tried to pull the meat off the bones. We kept jabbing the fork into what we thought were bones, but we couldn't seem to find the meat. Finally we shone a flashlight on the old bird and found out that we actually were poking the meat. The term "tough old bird" suddenly made great sense to us. His meat was as tough as his bones – so tough that we couldn't figure out how to eat him at all. After one last attempt, we declared the rooster inedible.

Bill and I felt terrible about not eating him. The Faiwol people, I'm sure, would have been able to gnaw on him and get some precious protein, but none of us were able to figure out a way to salvage this donated meal. What made our guilt worse was the knowledge that the villagers had killed the rooster in our honor – as a gift.

So we waited until really, really late. Bill quietly sneaked outside and threw the carcass WAY down the mountain. We felt sure some dogs were very grateful for their unexpected meal. Of course, we never forgot the event! I still have one of the rooster's tail feathers in my journal to remind me, should the memory grow dim.

What a glorious morning we had the next day – no rooster in the tree! I don't think we actually slept in any later than usual, but it was nice to wake up quietly with the sun. It shows God's wonderful sense of humor that when I began to write this book, I was sitting in my office in Belize, where I could always hear not one but several roosters crowing.

The fact that people still hunted and killed roosters with bows and arrows amazed us. They also used special handcrafted spears to catch fish. A group of young men came by one day to show our boys some spears that they had made. The fishing spears were different from the ones used to hunt animals. Instead of having a single point, these were often made of bamboo split apart into prongs, creating perhaps ten different points spread out like the underside of an umbrella. (Sometimes they actually did use the aluminum undersides of an umbrella, filing them against a rock, and putting a nice sharp point on them for their prongs.)

They would gather a certain leaf that, when broken up and mixed with water, made a cloudy substance that would stun the fish long enough for the fishermen to easily reach down and catch the fish either by hand or with their spears.

One day the spearmen invited Wade to go with them. Wade loves to fish and jumped at the chance. He had a great time, but found it challenging, too, as he learned that fishing in Papua New Guinea required him to be able to laugh at himself and have others laugh at him as he tried to catch a fish. By the time he came home, he had a new spear that the Faiwol boys had given him and had caught two fish! He later wrote his own article, published in a Wycliffe magazine, about his adventures.

35

Moving Down the Mountain

We had mixed feelings as we made our move down the mountain. The house we had been living in was in bad condition, and the living conditions on top of the mountain were very difficult. Yet, in spite of knowing how much we would appreciate the conveniences, we knew that we would truly miss being so close to our family.

We had decided to accept the Mecklenburgs' offer to let us stay in their house until we could fix up our own. The two houses were literally within shouting distance of one other. The Mecklenburgs' house had two bedrooms and a real shower system using the water from the rain tank. In no time at all we were settled in and found that we could still spend plenty of time with our family. We made a point to go up the mountain several times a week to visit. Our precious family came down to see us quite often, as well.

Ruth, Papa's sister and our aunt, came down the mountain once or twice a week to wash our clothes and help us in the house. She had seen the way I washed clothes and how they turned out, and she let me know that I wasn't doing a good job. I hadn't yet mastered the knack of beating my clothes on a rock in the river. We had a set-up for washing clothes but it took hours to do it all by hand. Ruth was such a blessing to us and took control of laundry for me. Her visits to our place were always special because I learned much about the Faiwol customs, as well as more about the language.

It rains an average of 330-350 inches a year in the area we lived in, which meant that it rained almost every day. The people called it dry season when several days went by with no rain. The Mecklenburgs had a rain tank, but the people who lived up on the mountains had to travel quite a distance, depending on where they lived, to get to water. Rain tanks were expensive and the villagers couldn't afford them. Instead, they would gather water in various containers, often in bamboo. Even when water was readily available, we noticed that the villagers drank much less water than we did. God had apparently adapted their bodies to the heat.

We had a week of very little rain. It was amazing to see how fast the ground dried up! Normally there was mud all around, but we could actually see cracks in the ground. The lack of water kept us from taking showers or washing clothes for several days. That wasn't a good thing when you had a large pile of sweaty clothes. We began to pray for rain, something I never thought I would need to do in the village! Nor had I ever experienced having to wait for rain to get water. Most Americans are very spoiled about water. We turn on a tap and out it comes. Now, though, I have problems leaving a tap running while I brush my teeth. Bill still turns off the water in the shower while he soaps up, turning it back on again to rinse. When you have gathered water or had almost no water for a period of time, you learn to appreciate it in new ways. Fortunately, our "dry spell" lasted for only a week.

As soon as we had rain again, Aunt Ruth came down to wash our clothes. While she was there she even washed our shoes, which were always caked with mud. I also realized that she didn't like the way I tried to wash the soot off my pots after they had sat on a fire. I used an American type of scrubbie to clean the pots, but Ruth used sand and a certain rough leaf and got those pots sparkling clean every time. I never mastered the art of cleaning a pot properly. I was always grateful for her help.

We asked Ruth that morning to have breakfast with us. I was making bread and spent some time showing her how to make it, as well. Because they cooked only on the fire, the village women didn't often make bread.

I took the opportunity to talk to Ruth about the bilums, or string bags, that the women used to carry vegetables from the garden, their babies, and a variety of general things.

I had been curious about these bags for a long time. I enjoyed watching the women make bags while they sat and talked and decided I needed to learn how to make one. I knew that the villagers got the "string" from a tree that they called a "tulip" tree. They would pound the pulp of the tree until it was flat and then lay it out to dry. Once it was dry, they took thin strips of the dried pulp and rolled it between the palm of the hand and the thigh until it became a string. They then took a piece of the metal rib of an old umbrella and pounded one end of it flat. (In the old days, before umbrella parts were available, they would use bones from animals such as fruit bats.) Once the end of the umbrella rib was nice and flat, they would punch a hole in the metal so that they could thread it and use it like a needle.

This process looked similar to crochet, which I knew how to do. I figured I could make one of the bags. In fact, I was trying to find ways to be more like the village women so we could identify with each other. At that time in my spiritual walk, I felt that I could "earn" my way into their culture. Learning how to do what they did was certainly much easier than making spiritual changes in my life that would bring me closer to them.

I asked Ruth if she would teach me how to start my own bilum. I think she was pleased that I asked and proceeded to demonstrate some of the basic stitches. I thought I was getting the hang of things, but once she left and I tried to continue on my own, my threads were a jumbled mess. I was too proud to let Ruth know that I couldn't follow her lesson so I went to someone else's house for help. The women there got me going again, but once I was on my own, I couldn't continue. I was frustrated. I realized that the ladies were doing the work themselves and demonstrating it to me rather than allowing me to try the work with my own hands. Once I did get my hands on the little bilum, I would have problems and they would take it out of my hands again.

It took a lot of trial and error and lots of visits to different women's houses to finally get something that started to look like a bilum. I was feeling pretty proud of myself until Ruth came down the mountain again. She said that perhaps I should work on a little pencil bag before I attempted to make one of the large bilums. It was a great day when I finally finished my little bag, capable of holding some pencils, an eraser and perhaps one exercise book. I eventually gave it away to one of my little friends, hoping that some day I might actually be able to make a bilum big enough to carry say – a load of laundry. I never accomplished that feat. However, looking back on the experience, I realize that God used my ineptness so I could spend more time with the women, learn more about their culture, and develop more humility.

36

Swinging Over the Fly River

Because of our desire to absorb the language and spend more time with the people, we thought we should venture out to where they spent most of their day – their gardens. We knew that the majority of the gardens were situated across the Fly River, but we figured since the villagers made the trip almost every day, it wouldn't be too hard to get there.

On our initial flight into the village, we had flown over the Fly River and noticed its great beauty. From the Mecklenburgs' house we could see only a small part of the river but we could hear its rushing water. It always sounded inviting. Frank had told us about a great picnic spot, which also sounded inviting. A picnic would be a good time together as a family and allow us some time with the people, too.

One morning we decided to make the hike to the picnic spot. We didn't travel as light as the nationals did, however. They went to their gardens carrying only a few things in their bilums. The women always carried much more than did the men. As for our family, we all had backpacks full of the things most Americans take when they hike – insect repellent, water bottles, snacks, binoculars, cameras, and sunscreen, to name a few.

Bill and the boys each had full backpacks. I had a small one – just the opposite of the Faiwol people's practices. Wade had even folded up an old air mattress and stuck it in his backpack, determined to float down part of the river. I've often wondered what the people thought when they saw us going on what, for them, was an everyday trip. Did they wonder why I carried almost nothing? Did they wonder why Bill and the boys carried so much? Did they think I was lazy?

The first part of our trip took us down the back side of the airstrip in the open sun. Then we passed through an area of low trees that formed an arbor above sandy soil. We called this place "Hobbitville"! Hobbitville with its cool, lush greenery provided a delightful shelter from the hot sun. After going through this peaceful, cool place, we arrived at the edge of the mountain and were surprised to see that we were facing a steep descent almost straight down to the Fly River.

We stood at the edge of the cliff for a few minutes, trying to figure out the best way to start down. The area was muddy and slippery, and it took quite a while to get down the slope. There were small, level areas mixed with nearly vertical portions where we had to hang onto rocks and roots as we made our way. All the way down, I thought about the fact that we would eventually have to climb back up!

After climbing down the slick, steep cliff and working our way through the thick brush, we looked out and up and saw the cane bridge for the first time. Frank had told us that the people went across this bridge almost every day to get to their gardens, but I hadn't imagined anything like this. The reason the gardens were on the other side of the bridge was to keep out the pigs that roamed loose in the village and were very destructive to growing things. Once I got a real look at the bridge, I knew right away why no pig would ever cross it! Instantly, I feared I would never make it across, either. Hanging about 20 feet in the air, it spanned about 200 feet of the rapidly moving river. You walked on a steel rod perhaps two inches in diameter while holding onto a pair of one-inch steel cables. At one-foot intervals, were bamboo strips that connected the hand cables to the foot cable. These bamboo strips connecting the handrails and the foot path were supposedly there to hold the handrails in place. However, many of the bamboo strips had torn and left large gaps. This was extremely frightening to me. I balked!

One of our boys crossed first and began to coax me across. As I took my first few steps, I remember thinking that this wasn't as bad as I had expected. Seconds later I changed my mind. First, the bridge began to sway. I noticed that the bamboo straps were getting scarcer. I hooked my arm pits over the handrails, thinking that if I began to lose my balance, I could catch myself.

About a third of the way over, I made the mistake of looking down. What a sensation! Looking down and seeing white water moving so rapidly under the bridge gave me the sense that the bridge itself was moving downriver! I did not want to continue, and called out to Wade on the other side to tell him I was turning around. Imagine standing on a tight-rope with your arm pits clinched over two guy wires and trying to pivot and head in the opposite direction. I realize there are circus performers who make a living doing that, but I am no acrobat. It didn't take me long to realize that I wasn't going to be able to turn around, either.

Bill, who was still at the base of the bridge, by the bank, was unaware of my dilemma. He was yelling at me and motioning that he wanted to take my picture. He even had the nerve to ask me to wave! There was no way I was going to lift my arms off that handrail (feeble as it was) to wave. I finally managed a weak salute without relaxing the death grip my armpits had on the handrail.

My focus was once again on crossing the bridge. I kept my eyes fixed on Wade and took one heart-stammering step at a time. Finally, I made it, greatly relieved and proud of myself. Now I could enjoy taking the time to watch Chris and Bill make their way across. Of course, if they had any fears about the crossing, they wouldn't admit it. Once we were all safely across, the reality of what was ahead hit me! I was going to have to re-cross that awful bridge to get home. I tried not to think about it as we continued on the rest of our adventure.

We had left the house around 9:15 in the morning and it had taken us about one and a half hours just to get to the bridge. We were somewhat concerned that we hadn't traveled very far yet. We knew that it was still a good distance to our picnic site.

Most of our walk was along the edge of the water where we had to climb over large boulders and gigantic fallen trees. Further along was a massive black rock that rose up on the side of the trail. As we got closer, we could see various species of beautiful butterflies perched on the rock, sunning themselves. We stopped to watch for a while, and later named that area Butterfly Rock.

Bill and I both jumped at one point, thinking we were being stung by bees. We realized that we had brushed against a plant the local people called salat, whose nettles feel just like a bee sting. The stinging sensation finally stopped. We examined the plant closely so we could avoid it in the future, then continued our walk for another 45 minutes to a really great sandy swimming spot. Wade pulled the air mattress out and blew it up, and we all enjoyed riding the rapids for a while. At one point we looked up to see several Faiwol men standing on the bank watching. I'm sure they found us entertaining and often downright crazy.

Our family had been alone together almost the whole day and we'd had a great time. Wade fished for a while but had no luck. Off and on, I thought about re-crossing the river. I asked Bill if he knew of any other way that we might return. We determined to look for a shallow place to cross on our return to the infamous cane bridge.

At 1:30 we started home. As we hiked, I scanned the whole area constantly, looking for a shallow spot but never finding it. Hiking fairly quickly, we reached the bridge without finding an alternative, and I knew I would have to re-cross it. Once I accepted that fact, I decided I would rather be the first one to cross and get it over with. I actually didn't do too badly. I simply kept my eyes focused on the other side. Hmmm.....focus must be important.

After we all crossed, we began the long climb back up the mountain and back to our house. The afternoon was extremely hot. I imagine the round trip we took that day was only four miles long, but much of it was spent climbing up, down or over some obstacle along the way. Perhaps half the trip had been on level ground. I was grateful to discover it was easier for me to climb up than down. At least going up, I could grab onto roots and rocks to help me.

Throughout the day, Bill made sure I drank plenty of water, but he hadn't had very much himself. Back at home, he admitted that he wasn't feeling very well, and announced he would never make that trip again. I was surprised to hear him say so because he was much better at hiking than I. I think he was suffering from heat exhaustion. Eventually, we did make the trip several times more, but we always made sure to take along plenty of water.

37

Learning to Laugh at Ourselves

Another trip to the gardens proved to be even more difficult for me. We were trying to get to the village of Dumanak that we heard was about a half-day's walk from our own village. We wanted to talk to the people there about possibly sending a teacher for the literacy training.

With a guide to help us, we started out on the same path to get to the Fly River but we needed to continue on for quite a way. Of course, that meant crossing the cane bridge again, but I was getting much better at it by this time.

On the way to the village, we went through the bush rather than along the river. The advantage was that this time, we were in the shade. The disadvantage was that we had to constantly cross over those slick one-log bridges and climb over fallen trees so large in diameter that we literally had to hike ourselves up and over the trunk to get across and back onto the path.

During our walk, our guide pointed out a particular tree, and told us it was a tulip tree. I got pretty excited because I knew that this was the kind of tree that the women used the pulp from to make their bilums. They had told me that tulip trees were difficult to find.

We talked to the guide for a while in our awful Pidgin English trying to determine if he was pointing to the very large tree in front of us or a large vine wrapping itself around the tree. We were both pretty sure he was talking about the thick vine, and told the guide that we wanted to stop at this tree on the way back, cut down the vine, and carry it back to the village.

I can't even imagine what we were thinking. It was all we could do to keep hiking, much less haul a large vine behind us on the way back. In fact, we were both so slow (particularly me) that we finally realized we couldn't possibly make it to Dumanak and back before dark, and that we had to turn around.

On the way back, this sweet, patient man was careful to point out the tree to us. Bill took out his pocket knife. The guide, who had never questioned who would carry this thing back, told Bill that he wouldn't be able to cut the tree down with the pocket knife! Bill told him he had a saw blade on the knife. At that, the guide stepped back to watch the show.

When Bill began to saw the vine, the guide stopped him again. He pointed to the massive tree and said, "That is the tulip tree." We all began to laugh. We assured him we would just leave the tree alone. I'm sure he readily agreed with us, and that he still tells that story back in Olsobip – about the two missionaries trying to cut down a huge tree with only a pocket knife!

As we continued toward home, the guide took us back a different way than we had come. Instead of walking through the forest, he was now taking us along the water's edge, probably because I had whined so much as I scooted across each log crossing on the first leg of the trip.

At first, I thought it was great that we were coming back on the water's edge because there were fewer large tree trunks to navigate, but I soon realized that we were now in the hot, open sun. Bill and I began to suffer from the heat. It's still funny to think about how the Faiwol people made that trip several times a week to get to their gardens, coming back with their bilums full of vegetables, and barely breaking a sweat.

I got hotter and hotter and when we FINALLY reached the cane bridge just before the steep climb back into our village, I realized that I was way over-heated. From my symptoms, I guess I would've been diagnosed with heat exhaustion. Like Bill on our first trip, I had a pounding headache and was very dizzy. I sat down at the edge of the Fly River and told Bill and this precious guide that I could go no further!

Now, imagine the scene. First of all, it was late in the afternoon, probably around three. It usually took us another 45 minutes or so from this point to get back to our house. It would be dark by six. I began to scoop water from the river and pour it over my face and head. I then told Bill that I didn't think I could make it up the mountain! I even considered asking him to go up to our house, get some sort of mosquito netting, and bring it back down so I could camp for the night.

In the meantime, the men and women of the village began to come back from their gardens. They gathered around me, probably wondering what to do. That was when I realized that no one was going to go home unless I went with them. About an hour had passed. I got up and started walking slowly. I crossed the bridge and took my time going up the mountain. When I was halfway up, I started feeling better and made it home without further problems. How easy it would've been for something serious to happen to one of us! How wonderfully God took care of us! The incident also showed me the love the people had for me. Though they never brought up the incident to me thereafter, I imagine I was the primary topic of discussion around the kitchen fires that night.

38

Ukarumpa

It was the middle of May. The Village Living phase of Jungle Camp was coming to a close. It would be difficult to leave the village, even for a short while. Many of our Jungle Camp friends had been staying in villages that they would never see again. We felt blessed to have been assigned to our particular village, with countless opportunities to get to know the people.

My prayer was that these developing relationships would allow us deeper access into the people's lives – genuine opportunities to share Christ – when we returned from spending three months in Ukarumpa, the Wycliffe center in Papua New Guinea. It was good to know we would be back. We packed up some of our few belongings and left others behind as we prepared to leave.

Even these temporary goodbyes were hard, but Bill and I knew that when we returned to the village,

we faced a separation I didn't know if I could bear –
from our boys. At that time, there were no options to
homeschool our boys, so they would stay behind at
the Wycliffe center.

Several people had described Ukarumpa to us, but
we didn't know quite what to expect. From the air, we
were surprised by how big it is. Ukarumpa has most
of what a small town in the States has – an
elementary school, a high school, a church, a clinic, a
post office, a finance office, a print shop, computer
center, some housing, and a community center. The
Wycliffe missionaries live and work at Ukarumpa as
support personnel, teachers, accountants, mechanics,
and carpenters, among other professions.

The town is almost a mile high in altitude, which
means the weather is much cooler there than in our
village – a refreshing change. In Ukarumpa we could
get fresh meats, fruits and vegetables. The large fresh
fruit and vegetable market was welcoming. The small
general store was usually well stocked, considering
how small the building was.

Most of the foods were imported from Australia,
but some came from the United States. The
Australians make many of the same products that we
manufacture, such as Kellogg cereal. Their way of
making them, however, is different. The box might
look the same but the taste can be quite different.
This even includes the candy bars. The Australian
version of one of my favorite candy bars, Milky Way,

tastes more like a Three Musketeers. The chocolate in the U.S. candy bars seems sweeter to me than that from other countries – but these were still quite enjoyable.

Several people in Ukarumpa had cows and sold milk. Among the many things we learned to make from scratch was butter from the fresh milk. To make butter, we just put the cream in a jar and shook it for about 30 minutes. Wade later made us a special churn that worked very well. Because of my city upbringing, all of these processes were new to me. I imagine if the reader grew up on a farm he might wonder at my amazement at being able to make butter.

In Ukarumpa, we worked with various people in the Literacy Department to prepare for our work back in the village. We remembered the advice from our leadership in the States about how we might need training in literacy. In our short time in the village, we had already found out that we would be helping quite a bit in the adult literacy program, so we set out to learn helpful computer programs. Some of the computer-based literacy games were fun. We made note of several that we could print out and use in the village.

In other preparation for our return to the village, we began drying foods in a dehydrator. I dried anything I could get my hands on, including strawberries, carrots, onions, green beans, broccoli, peas, squash, chicken and hamburger.

We also made preparations for the renovation of our house. Because it was so small, we didn't think it would cost much to carry out the few renovations we planned. When we got the cost estimate, however, we were amazed to discover that it would take around $10,000 to do everything on our list! A lot of that expense was due to the fact that, in such a remote location, we would have to fly in everything we needed. We would also have to pay the labor costs for some construction help. Bill and I decided that we would have to scale down our original plans, which was very difficult for me. I realized more and more how simply we would have to live from now on.

Our house in the States had been small by U.S. standards (about 1100 square feet) and very simple, but not this small and not this simple!!! I thought I would be adjusting only to life without electricity. Now I realized that it would include adjusting to living long-term in very little square footage.

We spent a considerable amount of time working with one of the construction missionaries to scale down our renovation plans. It took some doing but we finally figured out a way to make our house livable and, at the same time, affordable.

We got the expenses down to around $4000, which was still steep, but to take it down any further would have left the house virtually unusable.

39

Separation Tears

It was getting closer to the day when we would leave for the village again. We helped Wade and Chris pack up their things as they prepared to settle into the Wycliffe center children's home where they would live while attending school. I began to realize more and more the emotional sacrifice that it would require for us to leave them behind.

Back when we were in the United States preparing to go to the field, a few people questioned our love and commitment to our sons in taking them to such a remote place and then leaving them for someone else to take care of. I know now, looking back, that my ability to do exactly that had nothing to do with how much I loved my sons but rather how much I loved and trusted my Father who had called me to do it. Believing that and knowing that I was doing the right thing didn't nullify the fact, however, that this was one of the greatest sacrifices of our time in Papua New Guinea.

Leaving them is a vivid memory. The boys' house-parents brought them to the airport to see us off. I cried as I watched them from the plane window – watched them getting smaller and smaller as we took off. I told Bill my pain was so acute I felt almost as if they had died. I tried to find peace in the situation, knowing that we would be together again in about six weeks, but I could focus only on what was happening now – tearfully offering my sons to the Lord as a sacrifice of our commitment to serve Him.

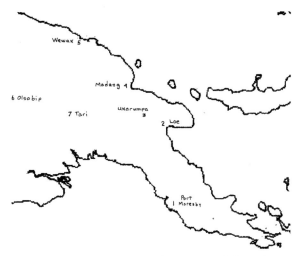

Papua New Guinea with most of the places mentioned in the book notated.

The island of Majuro – We stopped here for emergency fuel on our first flight to Papua New Guinea. Not very wide for big plane, is it?

193

Bill and I making our overnight "bush" house. This was the first time either of us ever slept in the jungle!

Landing in the village of Olsobip for the first time. Papa is holding Bill's hand. Chris is on my left and Wade is next to him.

194

Our Papa.

Our Mama. Don't you just love her smile?

*Precious village children. Note the young boy's
swollen belly – front left – most likely from worms.*

*Climbing the mountain to Kungabip (The Pig Place).
The ladies are bringing up their heavy loads. The
building on the right at the top was our first home!*

196

The outhouse – Note how it is perched on the hillside and that it had the handicapped handrails.

Chris and some of the villagers on our front steps showing off their handmade airplanes.

Our kitchen (hauskuk). Wade on the left with some visitors. Papa is sitting on the bench.

Chris is holding the rooster – our alarm clock! I am smiling on the outside but trying to figure out how to prepare this rooster for dinner! Mama is to my right.

I am going across the log "my way"
with Chris looking on.

Another log crossing with Mila. At least this one
was a little wider and had handrails!

The cane bridge crossing the Fly River.

Yes, that's me at the halfway point! Bill had asked me to wave! Notice the broken straps hanging down.

Our house near the Olsobip airstrip
before we worked on it!

Our house after renovations.
We loved that front porch, leaks and all!

Papa and Mama cooking in our front yard.

An aerial view of Ukarumpa – the Wycliffe center.

The Preschool

Bill showing off some of the newly translated Bible books.

Finamsep reading God's Word in Faiwol!

The singsing – celebrating Independence Day.

Approaching someone's house in Golgobip – the "Cold Place True".

Golgobip – notice the airplane wing being used as a washboard!

Inside someone's smoky hauskuk.

Our first Christmas in Papua New Guinea.

40

Remodeling our "Summer" Home

I was sad and quiet about leaving our boys behind for the first hour of our flight. We stopped in Tari to refuel. Tari was in the highlands and was the usual stopping point to refuel before going to the village. While the pilot was pumping the aviation gas, I stood outside and took time to pray and gather my thoughts. I felt a slight sense of peace. After refueling, our pilot, Randy, offered to take us to Tabubil first because of some flights he had to other locations. Tabubil was on the way. Going to Tabubil meant we could pick up additional fresh supplies. We gratefully accepted. Randy arranged to pick us up in two hours, so we used the time to run around Tabubil getting groceries. We bought carefully, knowing that it would be about six weeks before another plane came into our village with fresh supplies.

It had been a long day. By the time we got to our own village and carried all of our things to the

Mecklenburgs' house it was almost time for dinner. Frank and Charlotte were kindly allowing us to continue staying in their house while they were out of the village, since we hadn't yet begun the work on our own. We settled down for the night. Emotionally and physically exhausted, I slept well.

Feeling somewhat better the next morning, I was anxious to start work on our house – in part, to occupy my thoughts. There would be a lot to do to get our house ready for occupancy. Other than adding glass and screen to the windows, walling in a small portion of the dining area for a bathroom, installing indoor plumbing, and doing some minor repairs, we wanted to add also some silver insulation paper above the rafters to keep the heat down and put a different kind of insulation (it kind of looked like stuffed paper bags) on the walls. I hoped that these insulation changes and the windows would help keep down the bug population.

Bill and I labored there most of the day. I organized file drawers and Bill got our solar panel set up to generate electricity. We were excited about that! Eventually we would have one outlet in the house attached to the solar panel. It charged up our laptop and allowed us to run a printer on sunny days. When I needed to, I could unplug the computer and use the same outlet for my electric mixer to mix cakes and batters. The arrangement sounds pretty bare-bones, but it seemed sufficient to us.

Later, when we were back in the States on furlough, some people asked me if having only solar panel energy ever bothered me. I was able to honestly say that it had not. If I were living in a neighborhood in the States where everyone else had community-based electrical power and I didn't, then it would bother me. Or, if I had electricity and then lost it for a time because of a hurricane, that would be a problem! But we lived in the middle of a village where we were the only ones, other than the Mecklenburgs, who had even a solar panel. No, I never really missed having electricity on demand.

Few of the plans we made in Papua New Guinea worked out according to schedule. We learned this over time. For example, we were very eager to get our house "improved" and had great plans for our second day of work on it. Shortly after we began, the headmaster of the government school came over with his wife and spent most of the afternoon with us. They were very gracious. They had seen Bill with the wood and figured out what we were doing. They even brought their own hammer and helped out some. But because we wanted to visit with them, we didn't come close to reaching our goals that day. However, knowing the people and spending time with them was the real reason we were in the village in the first place. We often had to remind ourselves of that.

As we gained more and more contact with the Faiwol people, it became increasingly evident that we needed to concentrate on learning the language. A sweet girl named Jenny agreed to help me with my language lessons. Jenny was the sister of Peter, the health worker in the village. She had trained as a nurse and both she and Peter spoke some English. Jenny was very patient, giving me easy phrases to start with. I would take my simple sentences into the village and try them out until I mastered them. It was hard to get that singsong lilt to my words, and I left many people confused with my first feeble attempts at communication.

I looked out the window on one of our first days back in the village and spotted Bill setting off down a path. Several young children fell into line with him and the two closest to him grabbed his hands as they walked. When I told Bill how it touched me to see him walking and holding hands with the kids, he remarked that he felt the same way. We were building relationships. We were in Olsobip for more important reasons than just to teach literacy, although teaching them to read was very important. We knew our eternal purpose was to share Christ with the non-believers and to encourage those who were already Christians.

The Mecklenburgs had finished translating significant portions of the Bible, which they had printed and were being used in the village. We wanted to make sure that the people could read them. We met with Mila again to talk about the literacy program. He had devoted many years to promoting adult literacy in that area but was feeling very discouraged, overwhelmed with the task of keeping the program going. If that weren't enough, he had also been asked by several Faiwol villages to start preschools.

Because English is the national language of Papua New Guinea, the school system offered instruction only in English. However, none of the kids in the villages learned English until they started school. The villagers felt that if the children attended a preschool (they called it a prep school) that would teach them first to read and write in Faiwol, they could then make the transfer to English once they started first grade. Mila wanted us to start the preschools right away, but Bill explained that it would take time to get everything ready. We would have to make up our own books as well as train teachers. It was neither a quick nor an easy task.

Even though we had the title "Literacy Specialist" we felt far from specialists and had no idea at the time we accepted the assignment that we would be working to help set up a school! Neither of us had an education background. Not only was Mila feeling the pressure, but we were too. We had acknowledged the fact that we would be doing more literacy than management training, but now we were being asked to help not only with adult literacy but with the preschools as well. Once again God had put us into a position that we felt totally incapable of handling. Situations like this can be overwhelming and humbling but also exciting. It is always wonderful to see how God will work things out through us, in spite of our weaknesses.

Since the villagers seemed to really want the preschool and we felt God leading us to help them, we decided that the best way to start would be to concentrate, with Mila's help, on just one book. He wrote out a short story and we found someone in the village who could draw. Since Mila had to return to Tabubil, Bill and I started to work on the book alone, a project we called a Big Book. The Big Book contained a short story printed in a huge font on pages about two-and-a-half feet high and two feet wide. Later we would make smaller versions of the same stories for each child to read. At this point, though, we were excited to have a chance just to start on the Big Book. It was fun work, and we felt very encouraged when we finished the first one.

Time went by quickly, between the work we had to do on the house and for the preschool. That was good. I still missed Wade and Chris badly and needed to throw myself into productive labor. The work was going well.

41

Back to Tabubil

To work some more with Mila, we needed to go back to Tabubil and scheduled a trip there by plane. One of the men who worked with the literacy project, Amina, went with us because he had business in town as well. But Mila wasn't there to meet us; we found out later that his nephew had died. That information concerned Amina greatly; he wasn't excited about leaving us alone and said that he would stay with us, even walking through town holding Bill's hand – very cultural for that area but something Bill never fully got used to.

An Indian family who worked at the mine was gracious enough to allow us to stay with them. Mila had made all the arrangements. They had a television set that received CNN News, which we devoured for a bit, having been out of contact for so long. I have a note in my journal that Bill and I both woke up with diarrhea in the middle of our first night in Tabubil. This wasn't an uncommon occurrence. Diarrhea was something we learned to live with during our stay in the country.

Mila had also arranged for the Faiwol representative, Bob Buboc, to pick us up and take us to the meeting the next morning, so Amina reluctantly left us on our own. However, Mr. Buboc never showed up. With no transportation, we set out on foot for the meeting. Off we went through town on those hot limestone roads and finally made it, having walked several miles. Bob Buboc was there but never explained why he hadn't come to get us. We were encouraged by our discussions, though, because the leaders of the villages in the Tabubil area expressed their willingness to stand behind us and Mila and financially and politically support the work for adult and preschool literacy.

When our meetings were finished, no one offered us a ride so we began walking back to the house. It started to rain. Our road went from hot and dry to cool and muddy – muddy white! We had no choice but to keep walking. A very nice lady stopped and offered us a ride. We were extremely grateful and accepted eagerly.

We had been told to be at the airstrip the next morning by 8. There, we were informed that the pilot would not arrive until 9:30. Obviously, you never knew what would or wouldn't happen in PNG. Time wasn't all that important there, nor was it later during our years in Belize. Nevertheless, Bill and I never lost our own sense of time. We still felt the need to be at certain places at certain times.

Since the plane was delayed, we killed some time by going back to the store for a few more things. As we were returning to the airstrip, a man ran up and told us to hurry because the pilot was waiting for us! We not only had some groceries but we had bought a bottle of butane gas as well that was going to be delivered to the air strip.

The pilots weren't allowed to take passengers when bottled gas was aboard, so our pilot flew to Olsobip with our cargo and gas first and was to come right back to get us. In the meantime, a medical emergency came up that he had to attend to first. Consequently he wasn't able to pick us up until 3. Needless to say, we spent quite a bit of time at the airstrip. *Airstrip* is the proper word for it, too, as there was no terminal. There wasn't even a place to sit down. That is just the way it went in Papua New Guinea.

We finally got back safe and sound. We never minded waiting for a missionary plane when it was involved in a medical emergency because we knew how vitally that service was needed in our area. Normally, I'm not an extremely patient person, but I don't remember struggling with all the waiting we had to do in PNG.

It was good to get back to work on our projects in the village. There was a beautiful gorge not far behind our house that dropped right down to the Fly

River. Bill and a hired man worked hard to clean out all the brush so that we could enjoy the fantastic view.

Parts of our rain tank began to arrive on different flights. We were anxious to get all the parts so we could start putting it together and capturing the precious rain that would provide all the water for our house. One morning, we received a radio message saying that the last parts would be arriving that day.

When the plane arrived, we saw that the balance of the rain tank had come in but the assembly kit had not, so there was still no way that we could start to put it together. That was one of the frustrations of living in such a country. It seemed that you usually got "part" of something you needed rather than all of it. An integral piece of the puzzle was often missing that left you as helpless as if you didn't have any of it in the first place. Having all the parts from the rain tank would allow us to eventually have indoor plumbing. Then we could tear down our latest outhouse. It would be nice to see it go by the wayside, if you know what I mean!

School kids helped us carry home the parts that had made it on the plane this far. In the process, I learned more of the Faiwol language as we walked on the path. The children seemed to have more time and spoke more slowly and clearly than did many of the adults. They also were very patient.

On the next flight we received another valuable part of our home, a refrigerator. We had been asking around about affordable alternatives for a refrigerator that didn't run on electricity. We sent out a notice on the radio one afternoon and heard from an Australian missionary just a few days later who served in a village several hundred miles from us. He offered us his old kerosene refrigerator, a relic from World War II. He said he wouldn't charge us for the refrigerator, but that we would have to pay for the plane flights. That sounded like a good deal to us. We made arrangements and soon received word that the refrigerator should be arriving in our village the next day.

When the plane came, our first thought was: how had they gotten the refrigerator in there? Every passenger seat had been removed and the refrigerator took up every available inch. It was a rusty monster, requiring eight strong New Guinea men to get it from the airstrip to our house. Because the house was on pilings, we wondered if the fridge might fall right through the floor. It never did.

We soon discovered that our new refrigerator was cantankerous! This concerned us; it would defrost itself on a whim. Because it was so hard to get fresh meats and foods, we hated to risk letting anything go bad. The Mecklenburg's refrigerator ran on bottled gas and was so much more reliable than ours, so we usually took any frozen foods we had just bought in Tabubil or received on a plane from Ukarumpa and stored them at the Mecklenburgs'. It was a blessing

217

they had a refrigerator that worked so well. Ours never did work properly. We used it mainly to keep things cool – not frozen. That is, when it was working!

42

Home Shopping Network on the Radio

The longer we lived in the village the more we realized how important our support team in Ukarumpa was. Every missionary family in a village allocation had a couple who served as their support team. We had approached George and Debbie Bender early on because we had known them for quite a while. They were wonderful – a blessing to us over and over while we were in the village. Later, another couple, LaVeryl and Maxine Voss, filled their shoes when the Benders went on furlough.

Our support team contacted us by radio at least once a week to find out how we were doing. Periodically, they would also let us know a plane was coming our way and would then run countless errands to help us prepare for that flight. They would actually go to the market and buy things to put on the plane, get our mail and ensure it was on the plane, buy stamps, mail letters, coordinate things we might need from the hardware store, and tend to countless other details. Because it was often five to six weeks between flights, their ministry to us was very important and greatly appreciated.

One of my gifts is administration. I'm a great list maker! I remember planning and writing out our meals so I could give the support team our list for six-week periods of time. I would make up a master menu and break it down into the ingredients we would need. Ordering our food was almost a science as I tried to calculate how much flour, sugar, and other ingredients we needed. Of course by now, I had learned I was cooking for unexpected guests, as well. We had some wonderful plastic buckets with covers that we used to store our provisions. They kept MOST of the weevils out!

In between flights and fresh food supplies, we were totally dependent on our stockpile and anything we could supplement it with from the local trade stores in the village. Because we were so isolated, none of the trade stores were well stocked. We never really knew what would be there. I remember that once when Wade and Chris were in the village with us, Wade came in all excited because he had found a trade store with sodas! A few days later, we sent him back to look for more. Wade came home saying that the storekeeper had looked at him like he'd come from Mars and asked him if he thought he was still in America! We never again saw sodas in the village.

Several months had gone by, and I continued to practice my Faiwol. The greeting was actually quite long and went something like this – "Akabave; kiba ken teinbadave." Since the Faiwol language has some tonal aspects to it, this was said in a certain singsong kind of way.

I thought I had the greeting pretty well mastered, so one Sunday at church I excitedly approached the women with my newly learned phrase. I "sang" it out with a big grin on my face, but all I got in return were blank looks. The ladies were clearly trying very hard to figure out what I was saying. I said it again and no response. Then again! All of a sudden someone's face lit up, and she told the others what I was TRYING to say. They all got excited and immediately began to share their tok ples (Faiwol) with me, pointing to body parts and telling me the word for each part. While I didn't pick up many new words because it was all so fast and emotional, I could see that the ladies were very pleased that I was trying to use their language. I resolved to learn as much as I could.

I also enjoyed trying out some of my words on our new neighbors, now that we were living nearer the airstrip. Our closest neighbors were Ernest and his wife Grace. Ernest helped us quite a bit in the literacy program as well as with various projects around our house. Grace was one of the ladies kind enough to help me work on my tiny bilum. She was quiet and hard to get to know but willing to help me learn some of the Faiwol language and customs.

On market day, I was finally able to practice my newly expanded vocabulary with some of the ladies again. At first there were a few polite hellos, but when I struggled through the ten or so Faiwol words that I had learned, I found myself surrounded by smiling, animated faces.

Around that time we ordered a new four-burner gas stove from the Ukarumpa center and arranged to have it delivered. We got it all hooked up but couldn't get it to work properly. Bill tried everything and still couldn't get it going. All of a sudden two white legs appeared out of the bush along the trail to our house. An MAF pilot had landed and wanted to meet us. He was a whiz at fixing things and was able to get the stove working. Many people assume that the JAARS and MAF pilots simply flew us in and out of our villages, but they ministered to us in ways far beyond that.

43

My New Best Friends Are Only Three Years Old

I was beginning to communicate on a two- to three-year-old level which put me in good company with the younger children! I particularly remember one cute little boy. He would talk to me extremely slowly until I caught on to a word. It might sound like this: "K-u-u-u-u-u-ul   m-a-a-a-a-ak   t-ei-ei-ei-ei-ei-n b-e-e-e-e." "The frog is here!" But I did begin to learn. I wasn't sure how discussing frogs would help me evangelize, but I was confident in the Lord's ability to use all offerings!

In spite of our lack of confidence in our literacy skills, the preschool work was going fairly well. We had managed to get some more stories from Mila that allowed us to continue. Now that we had a few books started, we decided the best approach was to work on the curriculum for one full week of school, just to see how it would go. We had already decided that each week would have a theme. Some, for example, were based on indigenous animals or reptiles (frogs!). The language arts, math and science courses would all revolve around that theme for the entire week.

We also wanted to gather some appropriate music for the children. We knew that the Faiwol people love to sing, and often sang as they worked, whether in the gardens or on the way to them.

Though we found out later that many of the Faiwol songs were intended to ward off the evil spirits that the people sensed were there, we were sure that music would help the children learn and asked Amina to help translate a wholesome song for us. Amina began work on a song right away and really seemed to be enjoying himself.

There were usually plenty of kids hanging around so we left our house and went down to the government center by the school in the afternoon armed with some of the workbooks and games we had been preparing for that first week of preschool. We tried out some of the material on them, and they seemed to understand and even enjoy it! It is difficult to explain how "handicapped" these village children were. As they prepared to enter preschool, many of them were already seven or eight years old. Most of them had never seen a book or even held a pencil. We knew we would need to spend the first couple of weeks helping them to learn some basic skills like how to hold a book, which way to turn the pages, and how to hold a pencil.

It had taken about a week to complete the first week's curriculum, which included a few songs, our Big Book and the beginning of some typed reading books. We felt a wonderful sense of accomplishment. Now we just had to put everything together! Feeling a sense of accomplishment, we began to plan and work on the second week of the curriculum.

44

Doesn't Anything Work Here?

Around this same time, Frank and Charlotte contacted us by radio from Ukarumpa to tell us that they had finished the first translation draft of the book of Hebrews – certainly a cause for celebration. It was exciting to see each stage being completed, knowing that the Faiwol people would have more and more Scripture in their own tongue. It was always great to go to church and hear Finamsep using a new section of God's Word.

I was grateful that our days were full now. While the days of hiking and exploring had been necessary and fun, I can't imagine how boring it might have been to live indefinitely in a village without work to do. The Faiwol people, of course, worked very hard hunting and gardening. We wanted to stay busy, too. It was soon evident, however, that we needed to plan our time more wisely in some ways. We always got up very early to listen to the radio skeds (schedules), often welcomed early visitors, and then launched into our literacy work plus our house renovations.

This meant that sometimes we missed our morning devotional. Here we were, missionaries serving on the field, not spending enough time with the Lord. How much we needed Him then!

Bill and I usually had our own personal devotions, often sharing things with one another as we read God's Word. Sometimes we prayed together and many times we had our own personal time of prayer. I always enjoy praying with Bill. It makes me feel very secure and unified with him. Even if we have an argument, we pray. We have tried to have a family devotion several times a week with our children throughout the years. This often includes some Scripture reading, sharing about what we are learning and maybe reading through a biography like *The Hiding Place.* The children often take turns sharing the Scripture, and we all discuss what we learned. Because having a daily time with the Lord is as nourishing spiritually as eating food is physically, we felt a void in the village when we neglected to "feed" ourselves. I was thankful that Bill had recognized the problem and quickly took steps to make sure that we reordered our priorities. We thought we had learned this lesson well during our time at the Wycliffe Quest session, so we were surprised to see this happening again.

I had had a tooth filled just before coming to Papua New Guinea and now it was starting to give me some trouble. Already I was experiencing quite a bit of intermittent pain, and I wondered what I could do if it really flared up. One day, I bit into a cookie with a piece of metal in it! The only thing we could figure out is that a piece of the metal clip that closed the flour bags had gotten into our flour bin and consequently into that cookie.

Now I had a large chip in my bad tooth and no dentist or doctor to call at the first sign of trouble. Not only was there no care in the village, but often we didn't even have a dentist at the Wycliffe center in Ukarumpa.

We were also starting to have problems with our little laptop computer. We would turn it on and it would turn itself off. We took it apart and tried to see what we could do. We waited by the radio to talk with one of the computer technicians in Ukarumpa who came up on a regular weekly sked. On the air, the technician told us how to take the computer apart as well as different things we might do to try and fix it. Nothing seemed to work.

Finally, I decided to just think like a woman, since trying to think like a computer technician hadn't worked so far. I thought, if I were a computer, why would I stop working out here in the jungle? The humidity came to mind. I knew that a fan motor in the laptop had some heat coming out of it when the

228

computer was running and decided to make sure that the computer got turned on every day so that the fan motor could dry it out. It worked! As long as we performed the daily boot-up, we never had problems again. I'm not at all mechanically or technically inclined, but thinking like a woman can have its advantages.

45

The Original Mini-skirt

The Papua New Guineans celebrate their Independence Day on September 16, recognizing the day in 1975 when they gained their independence from Australia. We knew the celebration was coming up, but we had no idea there would be festivity in the remote area we were living in. We soon realized all sorts of activities were being planned because this was a government site.

We hung around the center the day before Independence Day to see what would happen. Quite a few people were coming in from the other outlying Faiwol villages. Some of us got the idea to make lots of popcorn so we could sell it during the festivities to raise much-needed funds for the literacy program.

We really had no idea what to expect. We had watched the villagers build a platform of rough plywood atop some empty 55-gallon fuel drums. Some posts had been tied together to hold up various colored tarps, which provided some shade. It looked like they planned to have some singers or speakers. This holiday was taking place on a Sunday so we figured that there would be a church service as well. We made sure to get there nice and early so we wouldn't miss a thing.

The opening ceremony began with the school children marching. The boys wore white shirts and dark shorts, and the girls wore white blouses and a beautiful bright blue rectangle of material wrapped around their waists to look like skirts. The speeches began shortly after the parade. Bob Bubac from the Tabubil area was there. Frank Mecklenburg made a nice speech and Bill was asked to say a few words, as well. After that we had a service in which the whole community participated.

Then the "sing-sing" began! A number of the people came out wearing their traditional clothes. We had seen a few people in traditional dress before, but never this many at one time. The Faiwol in our area, possibly because of the influence of the government site, wore a more "complete" (i.e. western) ensemble. Many of the outlying Faiwol villages still adhered to their original dress as was represented at the sing-sing that day. The women were shoeless, wore no blouses and had on very, very short grass skirts. Their faces, arms and legs were painted with white designs and they wore traditional necklaces made from berries that, when dried, were as hard as coral.

They wore large bilums on their backs. Both men and women wore elaborate headdresses made out of shells for the headband, adorned with cassowary bird feathers and various other colorful feathers.

As scanty as the women's outfits were, there was even less to the men's outfits: only head-dresses to adorn their heads and gourds shaped like long upturned carrots to cover their private parts! Some men wore a small bundle of grass on their backsides. The entire group formed a circle as some began to sing and others played drums. I began to imagine how life must have been when Frank and Charlotte had first arrived many years before. I had seen something like this only on a National Geographic special, and now here I was, witnessing it firsthand! I wouldn't have missed this experience for the world.

Fortunately, the women hadn't asked me to join them in the sing-sing. I smiled, thinking that if I had done so, it would've been just my luck for that picture to wind up in a National Geographic spread later. I could just see the headlines: "Amazing! Lost tribe discovered – with one albino woman wearing their sparse traditional coverings!"

The girls, however, did ask me to participate in the volleyball game. I said I would but was concerned about messing up their game on such a big day when I barely understood the "rules" yet. I actually made some points for the team when I served, and we ended up winning both games we played. I was grateful for another way to spend time with the girls, realizing they might not have wanted me around as much if I couldn't play. This was doubly amazing since I was still healing from the biking accident back in the States. I imagine, looking back, that some of this exercise was good physical therapy for me, especially for my wrist.

The celebration continued all day and well into the night, ending around 11 p.m. We had some sparklers and brought them out for the occasion, thinking the kids would really like them, but they were actually terrified at first. After Bill and I played with the sparklers a while, some of the kids caught on and had a great time. We did, too, although we were pretty sunburned from a full day out in the sun.

Bill's fingers were sore the next day after meeting so many men for the first time. This was due to their unique handshake. Men would greet each other by pulling on the knuckle of the index finger very quickly which produced a clicking sound. A few of these "handshakes" and your knuckles would start to protest. The next morning, we realized that the celebration was still going on. We figured we wouldn't get any work done anyway so we might as well enjoy some time with the people.

Once the festivities were over, we continued to celebrate because our boys flew in on Tuesday to spend their school break in the village. I had missed them terribly. The plane came in around 1 p.m. It was good that the kids were on the first flight because, as usual, the weather was turning bad. In fact, the MAF pilot who brought in our boys ended up having to spend the night with us.

Actually, we enjoyed having the pilots stay with us. We had little opportunity to spend time with other missionaries, and we often had a great time fellowshipping together. I doubt that any of those pilots realized how much their overnights ministered to us.

It was so good to have the boys with us again! They had missed us as much as we missed them. Later, as we had time to talk, we would find out that they had gone through some difficult struggles. Wade, in particular, had struggled with the separation. He didn't like the dorm style of living and the challenge of getting along with so many other teenagers. He had great house parents, though. It was more a problem of learning to live with so many people in the house. Six weeks of separation was long and, unfortunately, we realized that we had one more long separation ahead of us of almost eight weeks!

This was something we had to talk about and work on for quite a while. It isn't only the missionary adults who make sacrifices, but the children as well. We were grateful during the hard times that the boys had been part of the praying and decision-making process as we made our initial plans to go to Papua New

Guinea. I can't imagine how much more difficult, and perhaps destructive, it would've been for them to have been taken there against their will.

Bill enjoyed working with Wade and Chris on the house. There was still a lot to do. They began to line the inside of the tin roof with silver paper and the interior walls with brown insulation. Once installed, we could tell the difference in the house temperature almost immediately. Bill and our boys managed to sand and paint the window sills on the boys' first day at home, in spite of the rainy weather we were experiencing.

We had shipped our belongings to PNG in crates and decided to use them to construct kitchen cabinets. Some woodworkers in Ukarumpa had taken apart the crates, used the wood to assemble cabinets for us, then took them apart and labeled each one so that we could reassemble them. Parts of the cabinets had come in on various flights, similar to the way in which the parts of the rain tank had arrived. Once we got them all in and put together, we had a very nice set of cabinets thanks to the technicians at Ukarumpa who had coded them so well. Now all we needed was the plumber we had hired from Ukarumpa and the rest of our rain tank to come in so that we could begin to enjoy our new kitchen.

While we were working, we heard some heart-rending news on the radio. The same MAF pilot who had brought the boys into our village and spent the night with us on Tuesday had crashed on Wednesday. His wife and children had been with him and they had all been killed. This happened on a clear day, and there was speculation that the pilot might have had a heart attack. I had to grapple with emotion on two separate fronts: the tragedy of losing a family of fellow missionaries and the fear of putting my boys back on a plane again. There were so many potential dangers threatening us in this remote village. It would take every ounce of my weak faith a few weeks later to watch the boys fly out of the village, over the cliffs above the Fly River, and into the clouds.

Papua New Guinea is a great place for the Lord to put someone who is struggling in her faith. The very next day God would stretch my faith even further. That was the day He took away the radio microphone I relied on so heavily!

46

The "Cold Place True"

On that morning we woke up and started our regular routine with the radio skeds. This was our day to answer when the roll call came around. When the announcer called our names, however, and we answered that we were there, he continued to call. We realized that he couldn't hear us. That night I slept fitfully, wondering what would happen if one of us got hurt or very sick, since we couldn't get news out on the radio. Even though we lived near a government site, its radio usually didn't work either. In fact the government employees often came to our place to use the radio. My tooth problem was still a concern and I wondered what in the world we would do if anything else went wrong (splish splash).

It took some serious praying on my part to turn this over to the Lord. When would I ever learn that He alone was sufficient for me? I admit that I still have a lot to learn in this area, but as the Lord took more and more away from me, I began to learn that it was in Him alone that I should trust. Now I can look back and rejoice in the difficulties the Lord brought me through to allow me to realize that He is all I need. I'm grateful that during that time of not having a working microphone none of us was ever in any need. My tooth pain never worsened. The Lord provided.

We continued having extremely wet weather. On one particular rainy afternoon, two men showed up unannounced on our door step. Both were Faiwol village leaders who had hiked down from Golgobip, another village in the Faiwol language group. Golgobip was a short flight away but a long hike from us. The people in our village called Golgobip "the cold place true!" That amazed us – we couldn't imagine any cold place nearby in this hot country!

Both men were exhausted! We had often thought we might like to hike to Golgobip sometime but had heard differing reports about how long it would take us to get there. Seeing the travelers' condition, however, wasn't encouraging. We invited them in to rest. They ended up staying several hours because of the rain storm, and we had several interesting conversations. For instance, one of the men asked Bill if he thought the earth was round or flat! He really wanted to know. Bill, being the science lover he is, had a good time giving them a science lesson about the earth and how God had created it in such a unique (and round!) way. He drew the earth on a glass jar and demonstrated how it travels around the sun. The weary travelers were intrigued by the lesson.

It was providential that these village leaders had shown up on our doorstep. We were very interested in finding out more about the other Faiwol villages and also in finding out what the leaders thought of our being there. While the men ate the meal we offered them and rested, we talked about some of the things we hoped to do – starting a discipleship program and a Bible study. They readily gave us permission for both. They never told us what religion they practiced and never asked us what we were – they just gave us their blessing.

Even though our visitors didn't leave us feeling as if we would ever be able to hike to Golgobip, we received assurance in something far more important than that. We received their permission to spread God's Word among the Faiwol people using their own language. How marvelous of God to bring those men to us.

One early morning, not that long afterwards, three exhausted and dehydrated nuns showed up on our doorstep. The knee of one of the nuns was so swollen she could barely make it up to our porch. We couldn't imagine what had happened to the trio, but we could tell they were in some sort of distress.

It had always been our desire to have good relationships with all the church groups in the area so we were inwardly delighted to see these three nuns approaching the house. They explained that they were Filipino missionary nuns serving in Golgobip and had decided to hike down to see our area. It had taken them 24 hours! The Faiwol people had told them it should take four to six.

We invited the exhausted women into the house and offered them some rest and drink. It was interesting to hear of their work in the "cold place true." They were very pleasant and invited us to visit them some time. We all laughingly agreed that, if we came, it would be in an airplane.

Inwardly, though, we still had in mind that we would love to try it on foot. Perhaps we could hike up to Golgobip and fly back. Either way, we still felt the personal challenge to try. We picked climbing up rather than hiking down because we had already learned how much easier it was for the two of us. A climb offered surer footing and projections to grip. It was also easier on the knees and toes. We figured we were a little younger than the nuns and in fairly good shape because of all the walking we did. Perhaps we were a little naïve, too. Maybe we should have reminded ourselves of the other hikes we had made without ever reaching the destination.

We began asking around to see what our "family" thought of our making the trip. They suggested that we try the "half-way" hike. They told us about a stopping point, about halfway, where you could look out and see the view of Golgobip. If we got to that point and could turn around and come back in the same day, then we could likely make the full hike into the village.

We picked a day and made plans for the trial hike. A friend of Chris', Krista, was in the village visiting with our family for a few weeks. We had met her family when we were in Duncanville taking linguistic classes. Krista's parents were in the management training program. Now her family was assigned to the Wycliffe center in Ukarumpa. She said she was willing to hike with us. Wade had been asked by some of his village friends to make the same hike the next day so he decided not to go. The four of us took plenty of water and food, good shoes, and a lot of determination and set off early in the morning while it was still somewhat cool. Once we got up to a higher altitude, the temperature dropped some, which made the hike even more bearable. The heat and humidity always played an important part in our hikes.

I was frustrated every time we reached a summit of a particular leg of the trail and thought that we were getting to the top of the mountain where we should be able to look out to see Golgobip. Our original thinking was that we would climb the mountain to a certain height, follow the ridge until we might climb some more, and eventually end up at our halfway point. What really happened was that we would get up to a certain point and then follow the path back down and then back up and then back down and then back.......you get the picture.

The more we climbed, the rainier and foggier it got, and we began to get cold! Chris and Krista were real troopers and never complained. I'm the one who started whining whenever we would reach the "top" again only to look down to see the path dip and rise. I was beginning to realize why we were entertaining so many weary hikers at our house.

At one point we entered an area very different from the jungle trail. I can't imagine how it even got there. Instead of the usual rich black mud, the floor of this area was very sandy and quite pretty. We would later find out that, at that point, we were probably at the one quarter mark of our trip!

As time passed, I realized that I was holding up progress. I didn't think I could bear one more up-and-down segment of the trail and asked Krista if she was willing to turn around and go back with me. Was she willing? She led the way for a while!

We were starting to get pretty wet and chilly from the light fog. It was also very muddy on the trail, as it was on most of the trails we traveled. At one point Krista stepped into some mud near the root of a tree, and the mud sucked the tennis shoe right off her foot. Giggling, we dug through the mud until we found the shoe, wiped it off with some leaves, and set off again more determinedly on the trail towards home.

We got back and found Wade on the porch with the video camera ready. We told him that only the two of us had turned back. He pointed off toward the bad weather hovering right around where we had just come from. I prayed that Bill and Chris would be all right and that Bill would actually get to see the halfway point. I kept hoping, as well, that we women would find out that we had almost made it there. I felt that if we knew we had gotten close, we could prepare ourselves better and try the hike again.

Two hours later, Bill and Chris came back. Chris didn't look bad, but Bill looked terrible! Wade videotaped their entrance into our clearing as well. On the tape, you can hear Bill saying, "We've been to the bush and you don't want to go there." Now, we laugh every time we see that portion of the tape, but no one was laughing that day. Bill was really feeling awful.

Once we had time to take stock, Bill told us that the sole of his tennis shoe had come unglued shortly after Krista and I turned back. He took his shoelace off and tied it around the shoe to hold the sole in place. That worked somewhat but failed to keep the shoe tight on his foot. His big toe had already begun to turn black and blue. More alarming, however, was the fact that Bill said he felt sort of numb. I think he was suffering from hypothermia because of the cold. He was fine the next day, but we never again discussed making that hike. Wade cancelled his trip the next day, too – and he was in great shape! I guess we really scared him.

I asked Bill if they ever got to the halfway point, and he said they reached a place that fit the description.   Unfortunately, we'll never really know because the weather had socked in by then and he and Chris could barely see their hands in front of their faces. They came back not knowing exactly what they had reached.   It was only later, when we described the sandy area to others that we concluded that Bill and Chris at least came close to the halfway point and Krista and I may have gone a little past the quarter mark.

Chapter 47

Discovering a New Use For an Airplane Wing

When we did eventually make it to Golgobip, it was in a plane several months later. After experiencing the cooler weather on our hike, we took some light sweaters. However, Golgobip was really the "cold place true" as it had been advertised. We were extremely cold the entire time we were in that area. The nuns to whom we had offered hospitality on their trip down to our village took care of us. They gave us some wool blankets at night and we slept under them wearing every bit of clothing we had with us.

We decided to spend our time visiting the various villages. The Golgobip area was very different from our own – much wetter, muddier and rockier. We were constantly crossing boards strewn across trails to avoid having to walk in the mud.

The people were friendly and invited us into their hauskuks. I had become fairly adept at looking for a place to sit closest to the doorway when we entered to visit. If I sat too far inside the kitchen I would invariably start gasping from the smoke that filled the little room from the fire. I'm sure that's why so many of the people had lung problems. I noticed that the inside of the roof of their kitchens was covered in a black coating, which they used as their water proofing. Unfortunately, that same coating often made its way into their lungs.

We came across one village where the ladies were washing their clothes in one of the deeper puddles. I noticed that they were beating the clothes and washing them on something that looked a lot like an airplane wing! I asked them about it. They smiled and said that a plane had crashed in the area a while back and that they enjoyed using the wing to wash their clothes. I was grateful to hear that the pilot had survived, but couldn't help remembering that we were going to have to fly out of that place!

We were glad to have had a chance to finally see Golgobip and its surroundings and meet many of the people. It was exciting to explain what our ministry was and to encourage them in their literacy program. We wanted to make sure they realized that our literacy efforts were for the entire Faiwol language group, not just the Olsobip area.

The plane couldn't get into the village the day we were scheduled to leave, of course, so we had to stay an extra day. The airstrip was perched right on top of the mountain. You could walk onto the airstrip, stand at the end, and look straight down the mountain. It made for an interesting flight out, similar to what you might expect if you took off from the deck of an aircraft carrier. For the first few days back, we were happy to be sweating again and out of the cold.

Celebrating milestones in the village was usually interesting and challenging, especially since the people rarely used a calendar nor did they celebrate birthdays or anniversaries. In September, Bill and I had to get a little creative. The first wedding anniversary that we celebrated in the village was rainy but fun. We had some canned shrimp and put it together with some creative spices to concoct something we called Shrimp Creole. We also made some sweet rolls and opened some root beer flown in from Ukarumpa that we had been saving for a special occasion. We even had candlelight. Of course we had candlelight almost every night, but this night was special. It was even more special because the boys were there to share it with us.

The rain continued the next day, but we were still able to get some literacy work done. Once the weather began to clear, Jenny made it down to the house to help me with my language learning. A young girl named Marie came by with some flowers for me. I was delighted with her gift and had some quality time with her while she helped me plant them.

We decided that since the boys were with us, it would be a good time to go to the river again for a picnic. The trip to the Fly River now seemed like almost nothing after our last hike. So, off we went. We had a nice, refreshing time. The people seemed to trust us to travel by ourselves a little more, so we were often able to hike on our own. A side bonus was that we had plenty of opportunities to visit with those we encountered on the trails.

On the way back we stopped to talk to some people who had killed and were cleaning a pig. I never did learn to appreciate the sights and sounds of a pig-killing, but it was just a part of life for our friends there. We watched for a while and learned lots about the pig's anatomy – including some things we would rather not have known.

A plane was scheduled to take our boys back to Ukarumpa. The two weeks with them had gone way too fast and it was very difficult to accept that we would be separated again. We now had to endure the longest separation we ever had with the boys – eight weeks!

As usual, because it was so wet and rainy, MAF didn't get in until the next day. When the pilot landed and unloaded the plane, we found out that he had brought some of the furniture we needed – a desk, a bed, and more of the wood from our crates for the kitchen cabinets. He also had a new microphone for the radio!

48

The Country Club
Amidst Cardboard Houses

We had planned a trip to Tabubil for some more literacy work, so we were dropped off there first. The plane took off once again with our boys. We sent them off reluctantly as we were left at the Tabubil airstrip to wave goodbye.

Mila met us at the airstrip, and we went with him to his place in Old Wangbin Village, curious about where he lived because we had never seen his new home. As we approached his neighborhood, we realized it was a slum, a squatter area! Mila's house was like most of the others, made of plywood with cardboard filling in the gaps. There was a stream nearby that smelled of sewage – we never saw any outhouses. It was sickening and sad to see Mila's living conditions in Tabubil, especially compared with how he had been able to live in Olsobip, and it left us more determined to try to convince him to move back.

Mila had told us he could never live in Olsobip again. When we asked him why, he told us a curse had been put on him. There had always been conflict between certain villages in the same language group, even to the point of exchanging arrows. Mila was from a different village and spoke a different dialect than Olsobip's. We never heard why a curse had been put on Mila, but someone had reported to him that his life was in danger, and he had taken his family and moved them to Tabubil. We had lingering feelings of sadness about his place as we were escorted to a very nice hotel. It was humbling. We felt guilty about staying in such a nice, clean place after seeing his. To the best of our knowledge, Mila still lives in Tabubil.

It's amazing to look back on ourselves sometimes. There we were, thinking how much we had given up to live in primitive conditions and how "great" we were to do that. The majority of the world's people, however, live in those primitive conditions all of their lives. We saw it over and over again in Papua New Guinea and then later in Belize. I felt guilty for my reaction to my "difficulties" when I realized the wretched conditions of many people in the world.

Our literacy meeting was scheduled for 9:30 the next morning. As usual, things didn't happen as planned. No one showed up for the meeting, so at 11:30 Bill, Mila and I decided to leave, regroup and meet again at two. The meeting actually started at three and continued until five. In spite of the late start, we were encouraged. We were able to get a lot accomplished.

Some of the Australian women I had met earlier found out that I was back in town and invited me to a luncheon. That sounded nice except for the issue of my wardrobe. Most Wycliffe missionary women in Papua New Guinea have two wardrobes – their Wycliffe Center wardrobe and their village wardrobe. The Wycliffe Center, because it is in the highlands, has a milder temperature. At times, it gets chilly because of its altitude. We tended to dress up more there (not dressy, but better dressed). Village clothes, however, were usually made of cotton to keep us cooler; we didn't mind their musty smell.

The luncheon was to be at the country club. The country club!? I couldn't even imagine such a thing so near our isolated village. Even when I lived in the States I had rarely visited a country club.

I appreciated the invitation from the ladies but I also knew right away that my clothing wasn't suitable. I wasn't sure what to do. I had yet to meet a professing Christian from the mines, and I thought perhaps the Lord wanted me to spend time with these ladies for a purpose – but to go to a country club in those clothes? Well, that is exactly what I had to do.

I fixed myself up as best as I could. I put on my "best" village dress, and off I went. The outside of the country club looked like the other buildings the mining company owned, with metal siding and a metal roof. The inside, though, was quite different. Everything was tastefully decorated with pieces that must have been shipped from Australia. It was not overly luxurious, but it was beautiful. What a contrast with Mila's neighborhood!

I think the ladies were intrigued by our lifestyle. Several times they talked about coming to our village and even made tentative plans for a visit. They never followed through, however, because I couldn't assure them that they could get in and out of the village in the same day. They didn't want to risk spending the night in what must have seemed like a scary place to them. Although I lived there night after night safely, I couldn't convince them that they would be okay.

Most of the women I talked to at the luncheon were rather lonely – wives of the upper level employees at the Ok Tedi Mine. Their husbands usually worked seven days a week and many hours a day, sacrificing all that time to make a lot of money in two or three years so that they could go back to Australia and start their own businesses.

The women confided to me that times were tough in Australia for anyone trying to get ahead. Living and working in PNG was their way of earning a lot of money in a short time in order to have a financial start once they got back. I thought it very sad to sacrifice several years of health and family for this, but most of the women assured me that they thought it was worth it.

I felt sorry for them, though I imagine in some ways, they felt sorry for me, living in the conditions I did and in the clothing they saw me wearing. I believe I felt sorrier for their having to live the lifestyle they did to gain the money they considered necessary. It made me proud of my husband – and of my God. I don't know that many of those women knew their purpose in life, but God was beginning to show me that He had created me with a unique purpose in mind and, even though our living conditions were very difficult at times, I was living out His purpose. I knew I was exactly where God wanted me.

I managed to act poised as I had tea with these ladies of Tabubil. My grandmother would have been proud. She had been very keen on proper etiquette. In fact, for one of my early teen birthdays, she gave me a book on etiquette by Emily Post. I'm sure she never anticipated those manners carrying me to a country club in PNG for a luncheon hosted by Australians.

The ladies were very concerned about my living conditions and asked me if I needed anything. I couldn't think of anything. Someone mentioned she had some extra paint and offered it. I accepted gratefully.

49

Medicine 101

We returned to Olsobip the next day, Saturday, and as we entered our house, we were immediately met by a terrible smell. It took us a while to figure out where it was coming from. Though we hadn't ordered any chicken, someone had decided to surprise us with a gift on the flight that had arrived as we were leaving. Then, whoever loaded the plane packed the chicken into the drawers of the desk that was being shipped to us. Imagine our disappointment when we discovered this. We had lost out on some fresh chicken! There were fresh vegetables in the drawers also, but they were still okay – thank goodness. It was several weeks, however, before we got all the bad chicken smell out of that desk!

A few days after our homecoming, I remembered the gift of the paint cans from Tabubil and opened one. It contained one of my least favorite colors, purple. Fortunately the donors had sent white, too. I mixed a little purple with the white, ended up with a lilac that I could stand, and proceeded to paint the inside insulation on the walls of the house. I even covered up the huge, rusty kerosene refrigerator with the lilac. I would venture to say that we had the only lilac walls and appliances in the village.

A couple scheduled to help us with some of the construction on the house sent us a message that they wouldn't be able to make it, meaning that we had to do a lot of rescheduling. At this point, I have a note in my journal asking God to help me have a gentle spirit about the multiple delays.

I came down with a bad cold and sore throat. We kept a very complete medical kit in the village and had learned in Jungle Camp how to treat various problems, but it was always good to check by radio with some medical people at the center before treating ourselves. With our new radio microphone I was able to make contact with one of the doctors who suggested a certain antibiotic. Thankfully, we located that particular medicine in our kit, so I was able to start on it right away.

We not only used the medical kit for ourselves, but often for the villagers as well, who suffered regularly from cuts and scrapes. They often got terrible boils on their bodies. I was grateful that Bill and I stayed boil-free the entire time, in spite of the problems the boys had earlier.

Even though we were on a government site complete with a clinic, there was seldom a complete inventory of medical supplies in stock. Often the people would go by the clinic, find out that it had nothing to help them, and come to us. I usually tried to help treat the people who came to me, although by nature, I'm very squeamish about such things.

Sakiba came by one day with two terrible boils on his leg. I heated up water to soak them. That would help draw out the poison. I treated him as best as I could, washed my hands carefully and went back to work sanding and varnishing floors.

I heard something outside and stood up to look out the window. A young girl from the village, Josina, was standing there. She told me that she had come to help me with my work at the house. I was really grateful for her offer and invited her in. She didn't mention it to me, but as soon as she stepped into the house I noticed that one of her feet was terribly swollen. She also had a boil.

Her foot was so swollen that I couldn't imagine how she had managed to walk to our place! It still amazes me that Josina was so intent on wanting to help me that she had hobbled to my house. I would've been sitting in a corner somewhere, whining about the pain. Once again I was learning valuable lessons from the people I had come to serve and teach.

I seated her in a chair and had her soak her foot most of the morning. While I was comfortable applying topical salves and antibiotic creams, I rarely gave oral antibiotics to others because I'm not medically trained and I always worried about reactions. I was grateful a few days later to see Josina up and walking with a much better looking foot.

I was starting to feel better. The antibiotic I was taking for my throat was working. Sometime later, back in the States, I had to go to a doctor for another cold/infection and paid a significant amount for a doctor visit and another hefty amount for the antibiotic. I certainly am grateful that a doctor was able to treat me, but sometimes I long for that simple, inexpensive village medical kit.

Some of the medical conditions we faced were far too serious to handle ourselves. One such instance was when a young woman, Opa, became suddenly ill! Someone came to our house to tell us about her. We checked on her and realized that she was in tremendous pain. It was hard to tell what her problem was, but my gut reaction was that it was something like an ectopic pregnancy or a serious problem with her ovaries. We checked on Opa again around 5:30 that afternoon. It always got dark around six so we knew it was too late for a plane to come in and get her. We decided that if she wasn't better by the next morning, we would get on the radio and see if an MAF plane could come in and get her to a hospital.

257

Early the next morning, we saw that Opa was still in tremendous pain and very sick. We went back home to call for a plane. It took some maneuvering and lots of radio contact, but we did finally make arrangements for a flight. An MAF pilot arrived around 1:30 that afternoon and evacuated Opa for medical help. She returned to the village several days later, doing much better. I had been right about my medical "diagnosis." Her ovary had ruptured from an ectopic pregnancy. We were deeply grateful that God had used us to help.

50

Indoor Plumbing!

By mid October, we had gotten quite a bit of work done on the house and were ready to start on the plumbing. Because Bill didn't know much about plumbing, especially for a water tank, we hired a Papua New Guinean plumber from the Ukarumpa center. That meant that we had to pay for his round trip flight to our village, an hourly wage, and the cost of his food. That was part of what drove the cost of our little "project" so high.

When David, the plumber, arrived in our village, we were pleased to discover that the rest of the parts of the rain tank came in with him. We found David to be very likable. That was good since we would be working closely together and he would be staying with us. Not only was David a nice fellow, but he seemed to be very good at what he did. In just one week he was able to put our rain tank together and hook it up to the kitchen sink and bathroom fixtures he had installed. He even had time to build us some steps on the newly made porch.

David's expenses weren't the only costs we were incurring to get the house ready. We had to buy lumber, furniture, and other supplies. We had already scaled back our expenses to a minimum but we still thought we would need two solar panels.

After we ordered and received the solar panels, we found out that we were about $2,500 in debt with Wycliffe because of higher expenses and lower support. The panels ran about $500 each, so we decided to try to live with just one. Without ever having to make our needs known to anyone other than our precious Lord, we rejoiced when several people contacted us and donated money for some of our expenses in remodeling. It was a wonderful time of building our faith and learning how the Lord would provide for our every need.

I remember a note from a sweet friend in one of our supporting churches. She was remodeling her house at the time and was overcome by emotion as she thought of our trying to get our village house ready. She sent a sizeable check that helped us buy much of what we needed. I have seen the Lord provide for our needs over and over again. One of my favorite things about being part of a faith mission board is learning to rely month-to-month on what comes in. We learned much about living by faith for our finances while we were under Wycliffe.

Actually, trusting in the Lord for my finances has always been fairly easy. He has proven Himself to me in this area so many times that I don't struggle greatly with money concerns. I guess I had more trouble trusting Him about the ability of that one solar panel to provide enough electricity than about whether we would have enough money to buy it! By the way, that lone solar panel never let us down. We were careful about how much energy we used, of course, but never once ran the panel all the way down! God is faithful.

Though we still had a long way to go before we could leave the Mecklenburgs' house for our own, we felt we had accomplished enough to be able to start our first Sunday school class in Olsobip. How wonderful that God had orchestrated the pre-ordained meeting with the village leaders when they stopped at our house before they headed back to Golgobip. We felt it important to have a class for the children because they often played or slept through the service. We thought it would be a good way to make sure they learned some things about the Lord on His special day.

We met for the first time on Sunday, October 21, 1990, having no idea what to expect. About 30 kids showed up. I asked how many of them had Christ as their Savior, and no one raised his hand. I asked how many knew they would go to heaven, and no one raised his hand. We knew that we were in the midst of a ripe mission field that morning.

There weren't any books for the children so Bill and I shared our testimonies and a Bible story, read some Scripture, and then we all sang songs. Later, when our boys were in the village, they accompanied us with guitars. We found the Faiwol children to be very attentive. We also discovered that they had some head knowledge but little heart knowledge about spiritual things.

One thing that puzzled us was a group of kids who stood outside but wouldn't come in. Bill and I tried to coax them in several times, but they wouldn't budge. We asked the children in the Sunday school why the others wouldn't come in. They told us that the "outsiders" were Catholic and that their Catholic church wouldn't allow them to participate. Rather than looking at this as an obstacle, Bill and I decided to do whatever we could to make sure that the Catholics in the area knew we were there to minister to them, too. Later we would see God work in a special way in this area. In the meantime, we moved our classes out of the little building to a shady outside area so that all the children could participate.

After lots of work on our house, moving day had finally arrived. We were grateful that we had been able to stay at the Mecklenburgs' house while we were working, but we were excited to be moving to our own place. It'd been exactly two months since we had returned to the village from Ukarumpa. Not only did we finish moving our stuff into the house, but some men came down the mountain with lots of wood that we could use in building our bathroom wall and part of the porch and steps. This was one occasion when I was glad to cook for a large group of helpers. It was amazing to me how much food and salt they could put away. Fortunately, I had plenty of both.

Now that we were moved in, Bill and I wanted to try to raise a few vegetables and some flowers. The ground seemed fertile; some of the varieties of the flowers were gorgeous. I was excited to plant, thinking that we would have not only flowers but also a nice vegetable garden. Josina and two other girls came to the house and helped me plant peanuts, bell peppers and some beautiful flowers.

The people themselves used simple tools for their gardening. Even though some had steel axes, many of them still used stone adzes attached to a triangular shaped branch by bamboo strips. When they gardened they would usually plant string beans, yams, field corn, papaya, taro, plantain bananas, pandanus (a long blood-red fruit), peanuts, carrots, and several other kinds of root vegetable starches that we didn't recognize. They also planted pineapples which weren't native to that area but had been introduced by Frank and Charlotte earlier.

These sweet girls who came to plant were just three in a long line of volunteer helpers. It seemed that almost any time we tried to do garden work or harder labor of any kind, someone showed up to help. We thought at first that perhaps the people were looking for paying jobs but soon found out that they truly wanted to help.

One example was when Bill would go out to cut the grass. Of course there were no lawn mowers so all the grass cutting was done with a special curved machete. Bill would get out there with his machete and, after quite a while, proudly look over the small patch of grass that he had managed to cut. Around this time someone would usually come along, gently take the machete from Bill's hands and proceed to cut about four times faster. It was amazing and very humbling. The Faiwol are very gracious people.

As for our greatly anticipated garden, nothing ever came up! In fact the whole time we lived in our house, the only things that ever grew were things other people planted and cultivated. We never did learn how to garden in PNG even though we had cultivated successful gardens back in the States. This was always a source of comedy to us – the fact that if we touched something it wouldn't grow! Talk about black thumbs.

51

The "Wontok System"

Even though we didn't learn to garden halfway round the world, we were slowly learning more and more about the Faiwol culture. At Jungle Camp we had been introduced to the very complex, unique "wontok" system. If you were in any way related to someone, you were called a "wontok" (pronounced "one talk"), meaning that you talked the same language as he did and followed the same customs.

There were unspoken rules in this system. If someone was your "wontok," you had some sort of obligation to take care of him if he needed any help, whether in the form of labor or money.

This could put a big burden on those who made something of themselves outside the village, like government workers or school teachers. They were linked to an elaborate wontok system that could drain every cent they were making. Often they chose to work away from their villages to escape that pressure, since it was unthinkable to refuse to help if it was needed. Sometimes curses were put against those who did refuse.

We saw this playing out in the literacy program in our village. One of our jobs was teaching the literacy volunteers how to balance the books for the store that helped fund the program. In the process of doing so, we discovered two of the leaders who worked in the literacy store and saw mill run by the literacy project, had both "loaned" literacy program money to their wontoks. We realized that they felt almost compelled to do this, but also knew that these weren't their funds to loan out.

It was a difficult situation and one that we tried to handle delicately. However, as Americans still ignorant about many things in the Faiwol culture, we probably didn't handle it well at all. Bill talked to the men and explained that this money would have to be paid back to the literacy fund.

I don't remember how much either man owed, but I do remember that one man was able to pay back his amount fairly easily. The other man, however, owed a larger amount. It took him quite a while, but he did eventually pay it all back, little by little. I'm not sure that he ever forgave us for finding out about the problem in the first place and confronting him about it. As missionaries, we loved the people and loved to serve them, but sometimes still managed to hurt and bruise these dear people as we tried to "right" things.

The lessons we learned in Papua New Guinea have stayed with us for life and helped us over and over as we dealt with problems in other language groups, even to this day.

Though there were problems inherent in the wontok system, we realized there were also certain benefits. Because of our adoption into the tribe, we were considered wontoks with much of the village. This realization came to me during a conversation I had with Ruth, Amina's wife. During my visit with her she told me that she had planted a new garden with green peppers. I was really surprised that they even had the seeds in the village and became quite excited. Mine, of course, had never come up. I eagerly told her that I would like to buy some peppers when they were ready. She said that she would never sell to me – only give things to me. I was really touched. This meant that she considered me her wontok and took her responsibility in our relationship with us seriously.

We really felt closest to Amina and Ruth, who became our dear friends. We particularly loved their little girl, Rachel, who was about four years old. Rachel would periodically come down the mountain with her mother and spend the day with us. If I put on my flip flops, she put on hers. If I wore glasses, she wanted a pair on her face. She followed me around the house imitating me.

Rachel, however, wasn't used to an indoor bathroom and drew the line of imitation at the bathroom door. I couldn't convince her to sit on the toilet, so she would do her business standing astride on the toilet seat.

Another interesting experience with Rachel occurred one day while the two of us sat together eating bananas. I came across a section in mine with a worm in it, and quickly broke off that section and threw it across the yard. Rachel jumped up and ran for the piece, carefully searched out the worm – and ate it! She then discarded the section of the banana he had been living in! I still laugh as I remember these times with her.

Even though Amina was a good friend, our cultural differences could still make mutual understanding difficult. One day Bill was supposed to have a meeting that involved Amina. He waited a couple of hours for Amina to show up and finally walked up the mountain to see what might have happened. He was told that Amina had been out hunting all night and was too tired to attend the meeting.

While understanding Amina's need to hunt, Bill was frustrated to be stood up once again, and talked to Amina about it. Amina firmly but kindly told Bill that he had to hunt for his food. He reminded Bill that our food "arrived" on a plane, already packaged, but that he had to go out and find the food for his family.

The men hunted wild boar, cassowary, boa constrictors, and tree kangaroos. They also fished. This involved getting up very early and patiently hunting or fishing for hours to bring back just a little protein to their village.

Amina's gentle reminder always stayed with us and reminded us of the differences in our lives. We appreciated Amina telling us what he did because it was true – we could never truly live as the villagers lived while we had things so easy.

52

Special Times in the Jungle

Our Christmases in Papua New Guinea were all different, but I have special memories of our first one. A good friend of mine sent us a very small Christmas tree – probably about one foot high. It had lights on it. We were so excited that we broke family tradition and set it up a couple of weeks earlier than usual.

We had only the one outlet attached to our solar panel and didn't know how much power these little lights would take. Every night, once it was dark, we turned on our little tree. We would sit and stare at it for about ten minutes and then turn it off again so that we would have enough solar power left for the rest of the evening. I know that staring at the tree sounds silly, but our ten minutes of lighted celebration was very special to us for some reason. The tree was really our only Christmas decoration.

Using a catalog, we had ordered some gifts through a friend, so we had some special new clothing to give the boys. We put the presents under our little tree. Well, not really under the tree because the tree was so short, but the gifts were at least around the little tree. I feel sad that people sometimes have no special memories of Christmas because of the commercial way we celebrate it. If you ever want your family to get back to the "roots" of a real Christmas celebration, we suggest you drop in to Olsobip sometime!

Another special memory-maker was the time we spent with the stars and planets at night. The land was fairly rocky, and there were large boulders in the yard that I liked to call dinosaur teeth because they were shaped like huge molars. If we wanted to see the stars, we had to wait until the time around the new moon because the other moon phases, especially the full moon, were so bright that they illuminated the surrounding mountains and reflected light across the area where we lived. PNG moonlight was so bright that it cast shadows!

When the moon was at a lower stage, we would head to our one special "molar" at the side of the house. This particular boulder was large enough and flat enough for two people to lie down on. Bill and I would lie on top of the boulder and look at the thousands upon thousands of stars that could be seen in a place so dark and remote. It was a wonderful time to remind ourselves of God's faithfulness shown to Abraham as He pointed out the stars just before He made His covenant with him. When we read those Scriptures in the States and think of the stars in the heavens, we don't have a concept of just how many millions of stars are visible from Earth. In PNG, there were so many stars it was hard to see much space between them in the night sky. Through our binoculars, we could see thousands more. We could also clearly see the cloudiness of the Milky Way.

Even though I kept wishing that I had a star chart so that I could identify more of the constellations, our "uncharted" evenings left us with wonderful memories. There were many nights that we lay outside and enjoyed the handiwork of God.

53

Frustrations in the Business World

It's good that we had so many special memory-makers because we faced frustrations as well, especially as we worked with the literacy workers to help them establish businesses that would provide income for their program. The small literacy store, which was stocked with mostly hardware supplies, was the main source of income. Bill and I took the time to teach the workers how to figure out what their expenses were and then to figure out their markup so that they could make a profit.

I noticed when I checked in with Amina one day that some of his asking prices were less than the actual cost of the items. I explained to him that this wouldn't work – he was losing money. He told me that the people were angry, complaining that he had set the prices too high.

We asked him who was complaining about the prices, and Amina told us about yet another facet of the culture.

When people were upset or mad at someone they had a special way of letting him know. Let's say that someone was upset at Amina for setting his prices too high. He would never go directly to Amina or a member of his family and tell him that. Rather, he would begin to tell others. The news would spread from one to the other until at some point Amina would hear about it. It amazed us that years later, in Belize, we ran into the same thing. The Faiwol people and the Mayans are very non-confrontational people.

Amina understood the principal of what we were trying to teach him, but he also had to live with the people in the village. As long as we lived there, we never saw the store make a significant profit. Relationships were more important than financial profit. Could we perhaps learn something from this?

We pressed on – overseeing the store, developing curriculum, and building stairs onto our front porch. Meanwhile, nine months into our term in Papua New Guinea, I began to experience some strange symptoms. I ran a low grade fever almost all the time, which didn't really seem like malaria to me. Malaria usually manifests itself through alternate days of feeling bad. I, however, was feeling puny almost every day. This went on for several months. I even had a blood test done in Tabubil at one point to rule out malaria and other problems. Nothing was found and after several months, the fevers stopped.

In all the years we spent in Papua New Guinea and then later in Belize, we never had a serious injury or illness. I wonder now how God felt when I complained about little things while He was taking care of such major things in our lives. Sometimes I read about the Israelites and think how much they complained when God was blessing them all the time! I can only say, "Ouch!", as the Holy Spirit convicts me of my complaining in the midst of so many blessings.

Our house was coming together well. A group of men came to help us make a saksak (thatched) roof for our porch. It was beautiful and provided some welcome shade. We realized we had a problem the first time it rained – our pretty roof leaked like a sieve. The men came back and wove it tighter but it always leaked. In spite of the leaks, it was a great place to sit outside and meet with the people – as long as it didn't rain too much!

54

Preschool Workshop

We had made a lot of preparations for a teachers' workshop for the preschool and planned to hold the sessions in Tabubil. The Ok Tedi Mining Company offered us a place to stay and also invited the participants to eat in their mess hall. They were always very helpful, even printing some of the books we produced.

At one point we met a man who wanted his Lions Club to donate money for the work on the preschool. We didn't want any funds for ourselves and made sure to explain that to him – any proceeds would be used for the literacy project. The Lions did donate funds eventually, which helped us get quite a few more books published. Now God was using people to help us who really didn't know us!

The big day came and off we flew to Tabubil for our first real preschool teacher workshop. It was Thursday, November 22 – Thanksgiving Day in the

States. Of course, this holiday wasn't celebrated in Papua New Guinea, nor did we have an opportunity to celebrate it that day, which was typical for us on the foreign field. Thanksgiving is an American holiday. Through the years I would experience much homesickness around this holiday.

The workshop was scheduled to last two weeks. We wondered how many of the teachers would be there for the course, and whether we would be successful in getting everything ready. Again, we had no transportation, but by now we were in pretty good shape and didn't mind the walking, although the heat or rain often made things more difficult.

Bill and I were encouraged by how many trainees turned up for the class – eight teachers from five different villages. In the mornings the teachers wrote additional stories we would use for Term 1 and Term 2 storybooks and took turns reading them out loud in the afternoon. We could tell that they were having fun. The class was progressing better than we had anticipated. One unexpected roadblock occurred during the first week of our seminar: the mine went on strike! That meant that even the mess hall wasn't open for a couple of days. The first afternoon we dined on crackers, peanut butter and cheese. The second night, the mining company reopened the mess hall for dinner about 25 minutes late. The teachers and Bill and I were thankful for the regular meals again.

December 1 was Bill's birthday. I surprised him with a few presents I'd managed to buy at the grocery store, some nuts, chips and chocolate! We walked over to the only hotel in the town and had a nice lunch. The hotel had a small swimming pool where we had hoped to swim, but it started thundering and raining so we cancelled those plans. A wife of one of the mine employees heard that it was Bill's birthday and brought over a cake for him.

Sometimes, as we walked through town, people would call out to us. Many people knew us even though we didn't recognize all of them. Some were from our own area and had come to Tabubil. One man from our village, Henry, approached us late in the afternoon, quite drunk. For some reason he wanted to give us $10 Kina (almost $10 US). Of course, we didn't accept the money, and never found out why he wanted us to have it.

During the second week, we worked on the Big Books to match the smaller ones we had already been developing. Our excitement about our progress grew. The teacher trainees seemed to be getting excited, too.

Toward the end of the two weeks, when Bill and I presented what a typical day would look like at pre-school, something amusing happened. We had a timetable and all the information laid out so that the teachers could see the progression. Inadvertently, however, Bill and I got something out of order. It wasn't an important mix-up, but we wanted to have the teachers learn the order that was written in their books. When we realized what we had done, we backed up, explained our error and went on. Later, when the teachers split up into groups to make their presentations, every one, without exception, gave his or her presentation in the same order that we first demonstrated. The New Guineans learn by example rather than by books or paper and as far as we know still do their classes in the same "wrong" order!

Tabubil had a little church – if I remember correctly it was Australian Baptist. We were able to go there for a candlelight Christmas service. Even though this took place a few weeks before Christmas, it was special to us since we would be back in our own village by Christmas and there would be no special services. I was sad to see how few attended the service at what I believe was Tabubil's only church for the miners and their families.

Just a few days before we were to return home, we went to the Tabubil print shop and saw two of our story books hot off the press. We eagerly showed them to the teachers. All of us were excited to see the fruit of our labor.

The preschools went on to become very successful. I believe there were about 17 of them scattered across our language group. In fact, some very learned people at the Wycliffe Center later asked us all about the methods we had used in the preschool. We were able to honestly tell them that we didn't have a particular method, just a deep reliance on the Lord's direction. We are encouraged to hear that many of the Faiwol adult and preschool literacy programs continue, even to this day.

Once the classes were over, I was eager to get back home. Our boys were due to arrive in the village the same day that we got back, December 13. This separation of eight weeks had been even longer than the first – both were too long. We were anxious to find out how things had gone for Wade and Chris this time, since the first separation had been so difficult. In Papua New Guinea, we followed the Australian school year. That meant that we had our longest break – almost six weeks – in December and January rather than in the summer. We were all looking forward to the break and being together. The boys would start a new academic year when their school reopened at the end of January.

55

A Blue Christmas
In Lush, Green Surroundings

We got back to the village shortly before the boys' plane landed. We were standing by the airstrip waiting for them! It was amazing how much they were growing during these separations – both of them looked wonderfully handsome and taller.

In the evenings during the two weeks before Christmas, the four of us sat around our little Christmas tree each night, reminiscing about past Christmases in the States and enjoying our newly made memories.

On Christmas morning we delightedly gave our presents to the boys. They had managed to find some special foods that they knew we liked: granola bars, canned asparagus, butterscotch chips and nuts. Christmas Day was very special as we reflected on Christ's birth and the significance of why we were in PNG – to tell the Faiwol people about Him. Dinner was special, too: chicken, rice, carrots, asparagus and a banana cream pie. Best of all, we spent time talking and identifying what we loved about each other.

A few days after that special, blessed Christmas, I made an entry in my journal that surprises me now to read. I can see that I was suffering quite a bit, not really happy about the people I lived among, not happy about being in the village. I wondered at the time if I might be suffering from culture shock. We were approaching our one-year anniversary in PNG. Chris and Wade were home. So many good things were happening. Why was I still struggling?

Some reasons I could point a finger at, but there was nothing that I can honestly say should have caused me to be as unhappy as I was. At one point we found out that our mail was missing. By then, we hadn't received mail for five weeks, and now it appeared to be lost. I felt myself getting angry again over the little things. Why couldn't the Lord at least make sure I got the mail after I had "sacrificed" all that time in the wilderness and been apart from my boys for so long? I wallowed in my own wilderness at that time, struggling to be happy when I was feeling so much stress from trying to rely on myself rather than on the precious Holy Spirit.

Another thing I was dealing with was a deep sense of loneliness, even surrounded by a village full of people. I dealt with this periodically until I finally got to the place where I cried out to the Lord, asking him to take the lonely feeling away. I was emotionally tied to my extended family and friends in the States and missed them terribly. This was a sadness I dealt with constantly.

I'm grateful that I have never been prone to depression. I shared my concerns and loneliness with Bill, who tried to console me. Bill has always been my best friend; he still is. But I still longed for the like-minded feminine companionship that had surrounded me back in the States.

56

From Ashes to Feathers

Our first New Year's Day in the village was very interesting. As a family we stayed up the night before and talked about our dreams and visions for 1991. We welcomed in the New Year banging some pots and pans. I hope no one wondered what was going on! We really weren't sure if the Faiwol people recognized the change into the New Year because of their lack of calendars, but we heard drums most of the night.

The next day Temsok showed up. Temsok was very comical and almost always made us laugh. He wasn't much taller than four and a half feet. He was missing one of his front teeth, and displayed the gap almost constantly through the huge smile on his face. He looked even more unusual that day because he was covered head to foot in some kind of white powder!

He began to explain that various celebrations took place on New Year's Day. (I guess they somehow kept up with dates after all.) One of the celebrations historically involved covering themselves with ashes but nowadays, he said, they tended to use baby powder instead! I guess that was easier to clean up and probably smelled better. We weren't really sure what the significance of this was, but we were interested to hear him tell us about it.

Temsok invited our boys to go up the mountain with him to Loubip to participate in the celebration. It sounded harmless enough and both boys accepted. We weren't surprised when Wade jumped up to go because he loved to do different things with the villagers. In fact Wade was labeled "man of the place." Chris, however, was much more reserved and usually declined these types of invitations, so we were surprised and happy to see him accompany Wade. The three went off up the mountain.

We were a little worried about an hour later when we saw Chris running toward us, very out of breath and slightly agitated. We waited for him to catch his breath and asked him what was wrong. We were concerned that Wade might have been hurt, but Chris assured us that wasn't the problem.

It seems that Temsok and the boys climbed up the mountain and were taken to the men's house, a very unusual place. It was up on stilts, as were all the houses, but was a place where, in the past, the men would sleep during the extended ceremonies involving spiritism and the initiation of young men. The men of the village had assured us that nothing like that went on anymore but we were never really convinced.

When you approached the men's house, you noticed right away that the entryway was very small. Various things hung on the walls: bilums, pig tusks, animal jaw bones, stone axes, and other decorations. We were told that in the ancient days, skulls of the Faiwols' victims hung on the walls as well, but none were visible that day!

The men's house was being used as a meeting place for men only. Chris said that they all sat down and almost immediately started yelling, "Tokum, tokum!" Then they ran out of the house. Chris didn't know what "tokum" meant, but he ran out too. He later found out that "tokum" means centipede in Faiwol. The bite of the centipedes there can really hurt and make you sick for several days.

Chris explained that they killed the centipede and all re-entered the house. While the men sat around in a circle, a man brought in some enormous pineapples. Chris remarked to the man seated next to him that he had never seen a pineapple that large and juicy in the village. The man laughed and told him that these special pineapples were for the men; the others were for the women and children. Chris, glad to be labeled a "man," was enjoying himself and thought he could learn to feel comfortable with the men.

He continued his story. After eating the pineapple, someone else brought in another platter. Just about the time he started to lean back and enjoy the next course, he got a good look at the platter. It held a huge pile of some jiggly, white substance that he couldn't identify. He asked the men what it was and one of them told him quite proudly that it was the special fat from the pig. The entire platter was covered in pure white pig fat! At that point, the men began to eagerly grab at the pig fat, smiling as portions of it dribbled down their chins. Chris said that was enough for him. He jumped up to leave and ran all the way down the mountain, afraid that someone might try to talk him into staying. We laughed until we cried. We still laugh when we recount this story.

Wade came down the mountain later, at a slower pace than Chris had, with a new prized possession. It seems that he had taken his bilum up with him and some of the men decided that his plain bilum needed some dressing up. Adiok, one of the older men in the village, proceeded to put some Bird of Paradise feathers through the strands. The Bird of Paradise is the national bird of PNG and is protected. This is a fact that we didn't know at the time. We didn't find out until we went through customs in Australia on a trip back to the United States! The customs officers did, however, let us through with the bag when we told them the story of how we got the feathers in the first place. Once the officers were assured that we hadn't been killing endangered birds, we were allowed to go through customs.

We always thought it was important for Wade and Chris to feel that they truly had a part in the ministry that our family had been called by God to do. We felt that their role on the mission field was as important as ours. We needed help getting ready for the preschools that would soon be starting and asked Wade to help make literacy boxes. (He has always been good with woodworking projects – actually later building some furniture.) These small wooden boxes with handles would hold all the materials the school teachers would need. Some of the teachers would be walking quite a distance to get to their schools and could use their boxes to carry their supplies or store them on the site.

Chris worked on painting lap chalkboards. It would be important for each child to have a way to practice his writing. Paper was very hard to come by so chalkboards would give them a recyclable way to learn how to write. These two projects kept both boys busy during their stay with us in the village.

Sundays continued to be a source of blessing for us. I have always enjoyed the Lord's Day and taken pleasure in trying to set it apart. In some ways, it was easier to do that in our tiny village than it was back home in the United States, where there are so many distractions. Because we had been gone for a couple of weeks, we were anxious to see how our little Sunday school class was doing. We spent the class time telling the children about the real meaning of Christmas. They were very attentive and curious.

Finamsep, the pastor, hadn't shown up. The church members asked Bill to preach. Little did we know that in a few years Bill would be preaching every Sunday in Belize and eventually would be ordained as a pastor. This particular Sunday, however, Bill wasn't prepared to preach, nor did he know the Pidgin English language very well yet. He did know how to read Faiwol fairly well. He read from the copy of the Matthew translation and then spoke in Pidgin English as he explained the Scripture. I marvel at how the Lord often uses Bill to do last-minute, unexpected things. We've lived in third world countries for so many years that we aren't often surprised by sudden interruptions or challenges anymore. The Bible tells us to be ready "in season and out of season." All of us are to be ready. Always, at all times!

57

What Is That Man Doing In our Rental Van?

Because our family had struggled during our separations, we wanted to go somewhere for a family vacation. We decided to go back to Madang, the town at the base of Nobanob, where we did our Jungle Camp training. We had been in the country for a year already and it had been nine months since we had been back to Nobanob. We wanted to see our national friends again and take some time to rest and relax.

We were to leave on a Friday in January, but got the disappointing news on the radio that our plane had to turn back to Ukarumpa because of bad weather. Even though this was difficult in one respect, we always had a deep trust in the pilot's wisdom out in the bush and preferred that they be safe as well as us being safe. We settled in for one more night in the village, praying that we might be able to get out the next day.

I'm surprised by my resilience in these areas at times. Why is it that delayed vacations don't bother me much while too many bugs at night or a cat yowling out in the bush can make me so angry I want to pack and escape on the fastest airplane? I'm ashamed to admit how much I complained over such small things and how often I resented being right where the Lord wanted me to be.

Incredibly, the plane did make it to our village the next day around 1 p.m. We got to Madang around 4, heartily looking forward to our first vacation since arriving. We thought of Madang as being so civilized, and it's funny to note now that we didn't sleep much that first night because someone was beating a kundu drum most of the night. We had lots of noise in our little village, too, but this was a new noise.

The whole family enjoyed being in "civilization" again and being able to shop around. We stopped in a park which had a great diving rock, and the boys had a wonderful time jumping off the rock into the water. Water was always so refreshing in hot weather.

We ate lunch out the next day – a real luxury. The Gulf War had started, and I remember seeing a bit of the news at the restaurant – the first world news we had seen in a long time. I found it surreal to think about the war when we were so far away. Little did we know at the time that one of our older sons, Scott, would be in and out of that war before we even knew that he had been in it. It was good that we didn't know!

We also went to Nagada where we had originally swum our mile and experienced such wonderful snorkeling. It was always a remarkable experience to snorkel in Papua New Guinea, but we found it much nicer to be there as "tourists" without the mile swim ahead of us. We went up to Nobanob after that to see some of our friends and was-family, and enjoyed fellowshipping with each other.

We left Nobanob, on our way to dinner, driving a rental van. As we approached a turn at the bottom of the mountain, a Papuan man came running up to the van, yelling something at us. Before any of us could stop him or get the van doors locked, he jumped in! He was clearly out of breath and very frightened. We were just as frightened to have him in the van with us. He told us that he had been at the bridge where some men who had been drinking threatened his life. He was trying to get away. It was obvious to us that he was truly shaken, which helped us relax. However, Wade told us later that he had grabbed a tire iron from the back of the van in case the poor fellow tried anything! We ended up taking him into town and dropping him off at the police station. The unplanned experience shook us up some.

A beautiful spot called Sier Island lay off the shore of Madang. We had heard that for a nominal fee we could get someone to take us out by boat to the island to snorkel. We had also heard that there were biting bugs in the water, swarms of mosquitoes, and no shade. Still, it sounded like fun to our crazy American family. We figured we had already experienced most of the uncomfortable things PNG could offer and decided to go for it. A man named Saimon picked us up around nine the next morning and took us over. The boat ride was scenic and beautiful. The water is incredibly clear – hard to even try to describe – crystal clear all the way to the bottom with the most beautiful mixture of blues, greens and aquas.

Being able to see everything in the water can be exciting, but it can scare you at times, too. Bill noticed what first appeared to be a large gar swimming around. He watched it for a while and decided to get a closer look. As he got closer he saw that it wasn't a gar, but a snake. He also began to realize that the snake was aggressively chasing him! Bill got out of the water pretty fast!

We found bags and bags of nice shells, even a beautiful nautilus shell. This is a story in itself. While we were swimming around and shell-spotting, some of the village children joined us. One young boy – I don't remember his name – tagged along with us for a while. He could see how hard we were trying to find an unbroken nautilus shell. After a while he disappeared into his house.

Later, while we were swimming and enjoying ourselves, he called us over to look at a certain spot he had discovered and there, nestled gently in the sand, was a perfect nautilus shell. We are almost positive that he "planted" that shell, taking it out of his house and placing it in the ocean for our enjoyment.

Over and over again we experienced generosity from the people we came to serve, the so-called "poor" people. They might have been poor in material belongings, but they taught us so much throughout the years about giving and spending time with each other. Bill and I still have that shell and all the wonderful memories that surround it.

The island had offered us a beautiful vacation with the best snorkeling we've ever experienced. We never felt a mosquito nor saw a bug in the water. The people were friendly, allowing us to sit in their yards under the shade. We were the only tourists on the entire island. It was a wonderful, relaxing time away from some of the struggles of the village.

The four of us returned to Ukarumpa for a week before Bill headed back to the village for two weeks alone. I planned to stay longer in Ukarumpa to have more time with the boys. We'd spent quite a bit of time talking with the boys about how things had gone during our first two separations. They both enjoyed the school, but struggled being in the children's home instead of with us as a family. Wade, in particular, struggled with this. No matter how great the hostel parents were, the hostel simply wasn't home. Many missionary kids lived in the hostels and loved them, but many of those same kids had also grown up on the field and were perhaps better prepared.

One week later, a fellow missionary family approached us and offered for Wade to stay with them. Wade was grateful for the invitation and thought he would really enjoy living with them. Chris changed hostels and was content to stay where he was. Bill returned from the village a week later, spending a week in Ukarumpa, and then we both returned to the village.

Over time, Bill and I learned how to schedule our breaks away from the village – whether for courses or meeting with printers – so that we could minimize the amount of time we were separated from the boys. If we knew that a two-week break from school was coming up, we would make sure we were in the village two weeks before the break and have the boys come to the village for the break. When they returned to school, we might return to the Wycliffe center for a couple of weeks, which allowed us all to be together in the afternoons and evenings. This kept most of the separations down to two-or-three-week periods rather than a month or two, which seemed to work much better for us as a family. Both boys were happier and more content, and so were we.

Our first year in Papua New Guinea had come to an end, but the lessons were life-long. The next three years flew by, full of wonderful, life-changing challenges. Not many people have had the opportunity to live with a "stone-age" tribe. Although we still experienced stretching and difficulties, it was a season in my life that I will always be grateful for because I learned so much.

I learned that God loves me and had planned my life before He even created me. I also learned how faithful He is to lead us to what He wants us to do and to equip us in all ways to serve Him. He taught me how great a sinner I am in daily need of His grace. He showed me my sin lovingly and in such a way that I could easily run to Him for forgiveness. He taught me that He is everywhere, even in the uttermost parts of the earth ..... even in the outhouses we encounter in life. He patiently taught me that He wasn't looking for someone to perfectly fit a certain standard, but that He would always lead me and never ask me to do something He hadn't already prepared me to do.

As we neared the end of our term, we worked hard to complete all the literacy work we felt we should before leaving to go on furlough. We knew how important it was for the people to be able to read and write in their own language. Of course it was important for the children to do well in school, but the primary reason was that they and the adults would be able to read and understand God's Word, which would soon be in their hands. A few years later, Frank and Charlotte completed their translation of the New Testament as well as portions of the Old Testament and had a great celebration as they presented the Bibles in the various Faiwol villages. During our term we had often seen children and adults with widened eyes as they realized the impact of literacy on their lives. It is something I will never forget.

We assumed that after our furlough, we would be returning to the same area, even though we knew we wouldn't be living in Olsobip. The Literacy Department asked us to consider working in a more central location so that we could serve other language groups. We prepared to leave the village, knowing we wouldn't be back for at least a year. Bill and I had no idea that we would never make it back at all. During our furlough, the Lord called us into a different ministry. We accepted another assignment, this time in Belize, Central America. In a way, I'm glad I didn't know I was saying final goodbyes.

58

Back on the Mountaintop: Final Lessons

In June 1993, just prior to leaving for the last time, we made sure to visit the people in the different villages of our area, making the climb once again up the two mountains to Kungabip and Loubip. As I stood on top of Kungabip, looking at the outhouse that seemed to stand rather majestically now, I remembered my anger and bitterness when I first arrived. Now I had a chance to bask in the beauty of the area. The sound of children playing was music to my ears. I loved hearing their wonderfully melodious language. I also felt a deep, sincere affection for all the family members whose houses dotted the ridge of this mountain. What a difference a few years had made in my life and my walk with the Lord.

As the plane flew out of the village and made its last turn inside the fishbowl, I caught one last glimpse of the outhouse that had almost become my downfall in Papua New Guinea, but instead had become my tutor. Who could guess that a few years later a two-seater, bat-filled outhouse in Belize would produce a host of struggles that would bring me even closer to Christ?

If someone were to ask me if I would do anything differently, I would say no – other than to change my own sinful responses to the challenges God placed before me. But, if anyone asked me how my life would have been different if I had never responded to God's call to missions, my mind would immediately fly to Jonah's story in the Bible. Jonah was also called to a mission and also tried to resist God's call, to the point of running in the opposite direction. Although I never ran away physically, I sped out of control in the opposite direction mentally. Job would have missed an amazing demonstration of how God changes hearts – and so would I. I would have missed the richness of being on the mission field, a richness which greatly outweighed the difficulties. I had wonderful experiences and developed friendships around the world with nationals and other missionaries that continue to this day. I have a deep understanding of what God means by "all tongues and nations." God created a fervent love in me for other ethnic groups, which I now see being used in our work with ethnic groups in the United States. I know now that the church isn't just in Surfside, not just in South Carolina, nor even in just the United

States. The church spans the world and God is in control of it all.

I learned so much from the Faiwol villagers about relationships. I have a tendency to make too many lists, too many plans. The villagers were interested primarily in each other. Papa, whom I originally labeled a "gold-digger," may have started with the wrong intentions, but I believe his love and affection for us ended up being as sincere as ours was for him. Evidence of this occurred about two years after we had been living in Olsobip. Papa had been away, working in Tabubil, and came back with some of his salary. He came to our house and handed us some money. He told us that it was our family portion. He explained that he had handed out equal shares to all of his children. We tearfully and humbly accepted his gift, thanking God for allowing us to experience this adoption. Imagine how joyful we will be as we enter heaven's kingdom and realize the impact of God's adoption of us as His children!

If I hadn't gone to Papua New Guinea, I would have missed learning these valuable lessons. I would even go so far as to say that I'm grateful for the hardships I experienced in my early childhood. They made me who I am today. I can't say that I don't still suffer from some of the haunting memories of my past, but I know for sure that God has used those hardships to form me into who He wants me to be.

Yes, my life would be very different, perhaps unfulfilled if I hadn't followed God's will for my life. I don't ever want to be out of His will, even knowing that being there often requires some serious pruning and refining – ouch!

Perhaps you have an "outhouse" in your life, something that you constantly face that challenges you and your walk with the Lord. I encourage you to put this roadblock in our wonderful Almighty's hands to see how the outhouse in front of you can become a beautiful mansion. That is just what God did to my personal outhouse.

My experience in Papua New Guinea, and later in Belize, also taught me much about God's sovereignty. He has a specific love for me which showed itself in the way He prepared me, guided me, protected me, and taught me. The same experiences affected both Wade and Chris as well. Wade and his wife, Gina, have a deep love for our Lord and serve him faithfully in Siloam Springs, Arkansas. Wade's world-view is much larger than that of most men his age, and his faith has increased tremendously. Chris serves the Lord as a truck driver. He served the Lord in several short-term mission trips as a young adult and considers his current job an extension of the mission field. Finally, Bill, who was the first of us to desire a life as an agent of the gospel, learned many lessons that equipped him to evangelize wherever the Lord placed us: first in Papua New Guinea, later in Belize where we would adopt Juanaria, Virginia, Sonny, and Frankie; and now in the United States. Bill was ordained as a Teaching Elder in the Presbyterian Church of America in 2003. His commitment and faith remain a strong witness to our family.

70 44 26
33.3